Human Nature Mythology

Human Nature Mythology

KENNETH BOCK

University of Illinois Press
Urbana and Chicago

This book is printed on acid-free paper.

Library of Congress Cataloging-in-Publication Data

Bock, Kenneth Elliott, 1916–
    Human nature mythology / Kenneth Bock.
      p.   cm.
     ISBN 0-252-02072-3 (cloth : acid-free paper). — ISBN
  0-252-06365-1 (paper : acid-free paper)
     1. Philosophical anthropology—History.   2. Free will and
  determinism—History. I. Title.
  BD450.B539   1994
  128—dc20   93-24318
                                                CIP

For Margaret Hall Bock

I am aware that many of my contemporaries maintain that nations are never their own masters here below, and that they necessarily obey some insurmountable and unintelligent power, arising from anterior events, from their race, or from the soil and climate of their country. Such principles are false and cowardly; such principles can never produce aught but feeble men and pusillanimous nations. Providence has not created mankind entirely independent or entirely free. It is true that around every man a fatal circle is traced beyond which he cannot pass; but within the wide verge of that circle he is powerful and free; as it is with men, so with communities.

—Alexis de Tocqueville

Contents

Acknowledgments

My obligation is, above all, to the many students I have been privileged to work with on questions regarding human nature. Their contribution to this book has been greater than they might realize.

One version or another of the manuscript was read by Randy Baker, Stanford Lyman, Ron Roizen, and Colin Samson. I value their comments. Richard Wood's assistance throughout and, in particular, his guidance through the tangles of theological discourse are very much appreciated. Christine Williams gave each chapter a careful reading; her informed criticism has been most helpful. Once again, I am especially indebted to M. Katherine Mooney for her generous scholarly contributions.

Richard Martin, Theresa L. Sears, and Louis Simon of the University of Illinois Press have been unfailing in their expert professional services.

My work has been supported by funds made available through the Committee on Research of the University of California at Berkeley.

INTRODUCTION

The Human Nature Question

[1]

H UMAN DIGNITY has long been under assault in Western thought. People have been represented as powerless to shape their life expressions, to determine the course of their activities, or to make their own histories. Accounts of human weakness have taken four major forms.

First, human beings have been subordinated to a god whose singular and absolute sovereignty implies absolute human impotence. The idea of one omnipotent, omnipresent god who is the cause of all things and events and who has, therefore, foreknowledge of everything, has been used to brand any assertion of human effectiveness a serious heresy and a sign of sinful pride. This doctrine has been given awful import in Christian theology through the buttressing dogma of original sin: while God did create a man, and even in the divine image, the creature deliberately disobeyed and defied his creator and thereby condemned himself and all his progeny to lives of sin and futility, a condition that can be relieved only by unaccountable gifts of grace and never by any kind of human act. This total human alienation from meaningful earthly existence was portrayed most vividly by John Calvin, but the baleful vision neither began nor ended with him.

Second, people have been represented as pawns whose destiny is controlled by the operation of mysterious external forces. Suggestions that the stars affect our lives are an early and enduring form of this belief. Versions more acceptable to modern ears include the beguiling notion that History has a plan of its own and brings things to pass without, or in spite of, human intentional action. A variation on this theme calls on an invisible hand (now secularized) to produce ends that no one at all (not even God) had in mind. More recent ideas of fate or destiny are usually only rhetorical devices, residual categories to take over where rational explanation is wanting. Even then they are revealing survivals of an inclination to deny or to avoid dealing with human sources of human artifact.

Third, humans have been found to possess innate drives that direct their conduct, often without their awareness, along determined courses. The formal similarity of this thesis to Christian dogma is so clear that it, too, might be seen as a secularized version of the doctrine of original sin. That psychologists and biologists have so often accompanied their views about the mechanisms of human behavior with vigorous rejections of religion can be seen as not so much a case of the traditional conflict between science and religion as an in-house doctrinal dispute. In any event, psychobiologists and their various precursors in instinct theory can be regarded as influential contributors to the general belief that people are not aware of what they are doing.

Finally, people have been represented as creatures of a social and cultural milieu not of their own particular making or not of anybody's deliberate production, and thus as actors who play roles as puppets manipulated by forces external and alien to themselves. There are various forms and degrees of social determinism, ranging from the observation that any population is born into a formative situation that it had no part in shaping, to the view that the acts and thoughts of persons are no more than reflections of social and cultural circumstances. Often included in this general orientation are emphases on the unintended consequences of human actions, the absence of any effective social consciousness, or the presence of a debilitating false consciousness. Efforts of social scientists to point out the importance of social life in the formation of humans have thus led often to an exclusive attention to social structures and to a resulting disappearance of actual people from the scenes of social theory.

These four kinds of attack on human dignity are examined here,

in some of their specific instances, to call attention to their mythical character, to draw out their implications for human action or
inaction, to recognize their moral relevance, and to raise a caution-
ary voice about cloaked purposes in declarations about the nature
of people. Myths about human nature have proved to be potent. We
need to be aware of their sources, their meanings, and their typical
effects. And we need to restore an emancipating vision of humanity
that can reveal both the possibility and the inescapable necessity of
purposeful human action in the conduct of our affairs.

[2]

A revealing example of human nature mythology is provided in
speeches delivered by the president of the United States in 1981 and
1983. Addressing the problem of crime in his country, he argued
that criminal conduct is a result of the fact that people are "prone
to evil." Utopian presumptions about human nature, he warned,
have led to expensive government programs to eliminate crime by
improving the economic and social environment. We do this, according to the president, because we mistakenly believe that an explanation of people's misdeeds is to be found in the files of social
workers rather than in "the darker impulses of human nature." Philosophers, he noted, recognize this as the "phenomenology of evil,"
and theologians deal with it as the "doctrine of sin." False notions
about people must, he concluded, be replaced by these "absolute
truths" concerning human depravity.[1]

This case of human nature theorizing can serve, by its simplicity,
to reveal basic and enduring characteristics of the genre and to alert
us to problems and dangers in such talk.

One of the most striking features of this kind of discourse has traditionally been the absence of any evidence to support what is said
about human nature. The president's vague reference to philosophy
and theology is no more than lofty reaffirmation of the alleged fact
of evil in people. The reality of such evil is asserted with an expectation that anybody, at least after due reflection, is bound to acknowl-

edge it. It is something that everybody except the ignorant and the stubbornly naive knows. There is a clear suggestion of culpability in those who would deny it: in this instance, those spendthrift bureaucrats and do-gooders who are interested only in promoting their futile programs of social reform at a cost of wrecking the domestic economy.

The president's failure to recognize any need for demonstrating the fact of an operative proneness to evil in human nature should not be regarded as an oversight or as a consequence of his delivering a speech rather than presenting a scholarly treatise. The practice, as we shall see, is common in arguments from human nature. It amounts to mere postulation of inward human qualities—a sort of deus ex machina—in order to create an illusion of explanation for human conduct. A choice of a certain characterization of humans is mistaken for an explanation of their conduct.

The president's disregard for evidence makes the empty tautology of so many human nature explanations rather plain. Crime is defined as evil. Then crime is accounted for by a proneness to evil. The doing of evil is thus "explained" by a propensity to do evil, much as wife-beating might be accounted for by a wife-beating propensity in husbands, or, as in the classic example of tautology, opium might be said to put people to sleep because of its dormitive potency. Hegel made the point more elegantly: "all that is specified [in such arguments] as contained in Force is the same as what is specified in Exertion: and the explanation of a phenomenon from a Force is to that extent a mere tautology."[2] In the president's presentation we know of proneness to evil in people only by the exertion of that proneness—as in the commission of crime. It is simply redundant in that case to explain crime by proneness to evil.

The difficulty might be avoided by saying merely that we can expect people to commit crimes because we have seen them do it so much, but the argument from human nature will not allow this, for two reasons. First, much of the force of the case is then lost. When we say that a propensity to do some thing is *in* people, a part of their *nature*, we seem to be advancing a proposition that carries much more conviction than a statement of probability based on observed instances. Crime is a sure thing if it is in people, and the need for punishing criminals therefore seems more imperative. This has always been one of the most attractive and compelling features of the human nature thesis. It assures us that what we are talking about is real and unavoidable. Second, the bare fact that crimes have been committed leaves us, of course, with an expectation of crime but no explanation of it. Appeal to a force in human nature appears to explain crime and thus it stops the search for other explanations, a search that the president was not interested in pursuing.

By staying with the concept of a reified and potent human nature, however, one is exposed to the pressing question of how it is that a human proneness exerts its force more in some persons than in others, and in the same persons more at some times than at others. That is, if the frequency of crime we observe is not constant, how can we trace it to a constant in human nature? The problem suggests looking at something outside the human being, but that is anathema in the domain of human nature theorizing, as the president made clear in his rejection of environmental explanations of crime.

Variability in manifestations of human nature suggests another sort of problem. In our example the president, like other human nature theorists, is unavoidably speaking as a human being with the same nature he attributes to all humans. He is, therefore, prone to evil. How, then, can we have any more confidence in his declarations than in those of a criminal? Evil can surely express itself in deceitful and vapid discourse as well as in bank robbing. It is like the difficult case of the Cretan saying that all Cretans are liars. A way around this dilemma is suggested by the steady implication that the president was talking about "those people" when he spoke of evil in human nature, following the human nature theorizer's usual practice of excepting himself and a chosen audience from the debasing aspects of his generalization. Unlike some of his predecessors in this kind of discourse, whom we shall note, the president did not, however, try to account for his qualification for transcendent judgment.

His special attention to criminals in his analysis of human nature was an occasion for revealing another typical feature of this way of thinking—the habit of justifying public treatment of persons by endowing them with certain natural characteristics. How we conceive humankind both reflects and affects the way we treat people.[3] When the insane were thought to be possessed by demons they were chained and beaten. When people were seen by Machiavelli as prone to evil he could only advise his Prince to control them by force and fraud. So, when people who are judged as criminals are believed to be expressing an evil propensity within themselves, they must be locked up or otherwise punished, and that must be an end of it. Other options, such as social reforms aimed at reducing criminal activity, are ruled out as ineffective, just as other causes of crime are excluded because irrelevant.

An argument from human nature has commonly been used in this way to justify a proposed course of action and to exclude alternatives. It stops inquiry into and consideration of other explanations of why people act as they do. There is a finality about the appeal to human nature: "you can't get around human nature," "that's human nature for you," "people are all too human." The temptation is strong, therefore, to put into human nature whatever is needed to justify what you propose doing. Thomas Hobbes advocated the creation of a powerful sovereign state to restore and keep order in seventeenth-century England, and so he portrayed an unruly human being who made his program necessary. John Locke, a short time later, proposed a political organization of limited power, and therefore he pictured humans who were ruled by natural law and in need of milder governmental controls. We are under no illusions about Hobbes and Locke objectively examining the nature of people and *then* prescribing political institutions to fit. In the case we consider here, the president was obviously interested first of all in curtailing government spending on social problems. He justified curtailment by putting into unalterable human nature attributes that cause the social problems and thus make them impervious to political action. He had at his disposal for this purpose an old and widely accepted myth about human depravity.

These features of human nature mythology found in the president's remarks do not, however, reflect their most seriously demeaning implications for humankind. The disregard for evidence, the

logical problems, the dilemmas, and the spurious appeal in arguments from human nature are troublesome in themselves. And the
tireless reiteration of the story of human frailty is irksome. But it
is the charge of human impotence that is the ultimate affront to
human dignity. Men and women no doubt are guilty of crimes, however crime might be defined. But the president's indictment went far
beyond that. He argued, in clear effect, that there is nothing people
can do to alter evil behavior, either in themselves or in others. Nothing can be done because there is no accounting for the proneness to
evil; we do not know how it came to be there, and so we cannot know
how to be rid of it. We can and we must, to be sure, punish persons who are convicted of crimes, but that can have no effect on the
propensity to crime in human nature. (An argument that punishment deters criminal acts is hardly consistent with the proposition
that crime has nothing to do with the criminal's environment, that
crime flows directly from the criminal's nature.) The fact of proneness to evil leaves us without human recourse to alter that condition
by human action. This implication of human powerlessness in the
face of the human condition has been the gravest and most debilitating feature of human nature mythology.

[3]

As the above example suggests, declarations about human nature
are statements of belief about what people can be expected to do.
The question of whether we can construct scientific theories of
human behavior that could provide a basis for such belief should
not, of course, be foreclosed. Recent efforts along this line, however, do not promise imminent success.[4] As matters stand, we need
these statements of belief, these myths, and their historical preva-
lence testifies to the need.

Human nature myths, however, should be recognized for what
they are. They are not "absolute truths" or natural scientific propositions whose validity derives either from authority or from empirical
demonstration. Myths about human nature are *decisions* we make

about people: what they can and cannot do, their capacities and their limitations. They are decisions we make about ourselves.

This need not imply that the decisions must be arbitrary, that we have no basis for making one decision rather than another. Our devising or choice of human nature myths must be recognized as a moral action, but an action taken on grounds provided by considerations of human experience in following one or another sort of mythology.

The Western tradition offers us two broad kinds of human nature myths. They can be described as "closed" and "open" images of humanity.

The picture of human beings just examined is of the closed kind. It presents a human as invested with qualities that give rise to a certain course of action. If choice is possible it must still be choice shaped by a given tendency or proneness, which is unalterable by choice or by anything else. Closed conceptions of humanity specify restrictions on the freedom of people to direct their lives, restrictions that lie within people themselves. External restrictions can be seen in either the physical or social environment, but this also involves judgments about inherent human weakness in the face of such obstacles. The belief that human activity is subject to astral influence is an extreme case, but similar attitudes are reflected in alienating convictions about the economic system or technology or science or bureaucracy having rendered us helpless to alter a course of events that appears to proceed of its own and not of any human volition. The idea of human subjection to inner forces and the belief in our external bondage through unwitting creation of cages for ourselves are related facets of a closed theory about powerless and unfree human beings. This myth presents human thralldom as an inevitable consequence of human life itself.

An open conception of human nature represents people as both free and obliged to form their thinking and their conduct by their own actions in a material and a social world. The organic apparatus they bring to this task is seen as a given, because we know little, so far, of its influence in the production of differences in thought and action among humans. The human animal as such is distinguished

by this capacity and this necessity to form itself by its activity without blueprint or direction from any other source. Free, choosing,
moral human beings do not have a nature like that of other animals
—no set of regulators, directors, drivers, or selectors that conduct
them through their life situations. But humans do have a distinctive
nature (if we can use that rather vague term meaningfully) in that
they create by their free activity what is most important to them, in
a process of replacing or remolding now what others have molded
before. This is an emancipating myth.

Such affirmations of human dignity and responses to attacks
upon it have not, of course, been entirely wanting in the Western tradition. We inherit from classical philosophy, from pre-Augustinean
theology, from the Renaissance, and from flashes of the Enlightenment a solid foundation of belief in humans as conscious, rational,
active bearers of a comprehensible moral order in an orderly universe.

But we have been quick to seek explanation of our problems and
failures in what we *are* instead of in what we *do*. We seem wedded
to a belief that our situation is a consequence of our nature rather
than of our historical acts, and given to a mode of thought that
represents nature as necessary and history as mere happenstance.
As Montaigne and Tocqueville and others have pointed out, there is
cowardice in this inclination to shirk responsibility for our conduct
and to blame it on natural dispositions or circumstances beyond our
control.

A belief in and confidence in human dignity has proved, then, to
be a fragile heritage. In a swiftly moving world of discovery where
every aspect of the universe seems to be within the grasp of our
intellect, humans and the essence of their life have somehow eluded
the nets of natural science. And so human beings as active creators
of themselves have been passed by or denied as possible *subjects* of
study. Or only features of the human that show up as objects claim
major attention in the social sciences.

But even in that domain there are encouraging signs of a resolve
to accept people as effective actors, as decision makers, as conscious
architects of their lives, and as moral subjects. The following discus-

sion attempts to discern and to highlight such aspects of the humanist heritage and their recent cultivation.

In his *Essay on Man,* Ernst Cassirer called for a renewal of the
unified image of humans that once prevailed in the Western world.
Amidst growing signs that we are losing our nerve in the face of an
increasingly complex social life, we need such a restoration of faith
in human dignity.

CHAPTER ONE

Images of Adam's Offspring

THEOLOGY is the major source of Western myths about human nature. That is to be expected in a culture shaped intellectually by efforts to combine and reconcile Hellenic and Hebraic-Christian traditions, especially since the undertaking in its formative stages was so largely the work of scholars whose home was a Christian church. It is a curious and complicated story marked by the irony of a message of love and hope and freedom being transformed into one of so much hatred and despair and bondage. It is the history of a succession of elevating and degrading images of human beings, a history worth reviewing in some of its aspects because it can help us to identify significant features of later human nature mythology.

[1]

What kind of creature had God brought forth in Adam? The book of Genesis was hardly definitive on the question; speculation was invited. Modern historians of religion have discerned two sharply divergent views in the writings of early divines.[1]

One, represented by such figures as Clement of Alexandria, Irenaeus, Justin, and, especially, John Chrysostom, saw Adam's Fall as a serious lesson in humility for all humankind, but not as an event that deprived people of freedom to choose good over evil or that destroyed in them the power to nurture the substantial image of God remaining within them. Any lingering taint from earlier sin is cleansed, they argued, through Christian baptism, which enables humans (or at least a spiritual elite among them) to control themselves and their destiny in accordance with divine law, a law that people are capable of knowing and free to choose as a guide for conduct. For Didymus the Blind the essence of the Christian message was this: "now we are found once more such as we were when we were first made: sinless and masters of ourselves."[2] The point here was not just that people are good or capable of goodness, but, more basically, that they are free and able to choose what they will be and to so shape themselves.

The matter of human freedom was no empty philosophical concern in the fourth and fifth centuries. The claims of Roman imperial power and of church power were real and strong, and the question of whether people could live peacefully with one another according to rules of their own making was of practical importance for men and women in their daily lives. The answer to that question, and the way in which the answer was formulated, were to have consequences in Western political history.

The other image of human nature, which came to prevail throughout medieval Europe, was put together by Saint Augustine (354–430). It was a picture of almost total depravity on the one hand and nearly complete impotence on the other.[3] The qualifiers are needed because Augustine often granted a limited potential for human goodness, and he represented history as an education of humankind in the ways of righteousness. But his basic sketch of the human condition is one of bondage. Taking his own failure to conquer or control his sexual appetite as a model of both human wickedness and human weakness, he came to see an exercise of will itself as both evil and futile, thus laying a basis in Christian theology for the plaguing paradox of how one can at the same time be obliged to do right and be deprived of the power to do so—to be held responsible for doing evil when it is inevitable that you will do evil.

Augustine's handling of the problem is involved and full of contradictions, and theological discourse on the question has since grown fantastically complex. The concept of original sin is central to the Augustinian analysis. Adam's sin is interpreted as the sin of pride—a defiance of God's will and a bold assertion of the freedom of humans to do as they wish—but the fateful twist in Augustine's version is his assertion that all human beings descended from Adam bear the consequences of his sin as if they had committed the sin themselves. Faced with the difficult question of how Adam's sinfulness came to taint others, Augustine resorted to a biological explanation: the defect has been carried in Adam's semen. All humans conceived by semen (Christ, of course, is excepted) therefore have Adam's sin in themselves from the moment of conception. The mechanisms that might be at work here were not specified by Augustine, of course, but this strange argument prevailed in Christian theology for centuries despite the fact that it had no basis in scripture other than a vague passage in Paul's Epistle to the Romans (5:12). It was not the first, nor by any means the last, time that appeals to biology proved so strikingly effective in human nature discourse.

Implications of Augustine's doctrine of original sin led church theologians on occasion into extreme positions. The situation of infants posed a particularly difficult question. Were babes, or even unborn fetuses, guilty? For Augustine, that necessarily followed, and he took his opponent, Pelagius, to task for suggesting that sin in children consisted in such things as pettishness—their own acts—instead of inherited defect. He granted, magnanimously, that the crying of a baby is not a sin deserving eternal punishment; but that did not mean the unbaptized infant would escape "everlasting fire." As one divine is said to have observed, there could be no doubt that there are "infants not a span long crawling about the floor of hell."[4]

What could have led Saint Augustine to his views on human nature and why his opinions came to prevail over quite different Christian beliefs are questions that cannot be answered with sureness. Stephan Chorover has argued that such characterizations of human beings have always been concocted for the purpose of justifying harsh social and political control over people for the purpose of benefiting a ruling class.[5] While it is clear that human nature myths have often accommodated certain policy or action agendas, it is difficult to read Augustine's impassioned message and see it as nothing more than a plot to justify submission of Christians to political or ecclesiastical power.[6] Elaine Pagels is more persuasive in arguing that Augustine's picture of a fallen humanity in need of control only coincided with imperial and church aims and was not contrived just to further them. Despite this reserve, Pagels does not hesitate to criticize the extremity and the paradoxical nature of Augustine's argument, especially in its later anti-Pelagian forms. Her accounting for the more widespread and even recent acceptance of the doctrine of original sin depends on broader considerations of a common need or propensity in people for blaming their misfortunes on themselves—on their own wrongdoing.[7]

Whatever might explain the success of Augustine's bleak picture of humans, it became accepted church doctrine and more or less dominated European thinking for centuries. There were modifying influences, however. Earlier Christian ideas about human freedom and capacities did not disappear entirely and they were buttressed by Platonic and Aristotelian views as these came to be better known in medieval Europe. By the thirteenth century Thomas Aquinas could attempt a reconciliation of Aristotle and Christianity in which he "rescued man from the slough of impotence and depravity where he had been flung by Augustine."[8] Then, in the fifteenth century, humanists of the Italian Renaissance offered an eloquent defense of human dignity.

[2]

Although it is possible to find precedents for Renaissance ideas of human worth in earlier writings, the period nevertheless stands out in Western history for its vigorous assertion of a capacity in people to choose freely and rationally their ways of thinking and acting. There was a strong revival or rebirth of the classical belief in a correspondence of reason and order that could be grasped by human intellect and within which human agents could work effectively. How such an orientation was possible within a Christian framework still resting largely on Augustinian foundations is puzzling, but theological themes accommodate many variations.[9]

The importance of the human being was the basic message of Platonists like Marsilio Ficino (1433–99) and Pico della Mirandola (1463–94). Within a universe conceived as a great hierarchy or chain of being, humans were represented as center and microcosm, God's fairest creation and an epitome of all God's work. Human dignity in the sense of intrinsic excellence and elevation of rank was depicted as unmatched in the order of existence. The difference between humans and God was seen, of course, as immense, but the emphasis was on humanity's approach to divinity rather than on its humiliating inferiority. In both Ficino and Pico, however, human excellence is recognized as potential only, and given the fact that humans participate in all the orders of being they also contain a potential for brutishness. People therefore find themselves in a difficult situation—the difficulty of being human. This calls for action on their part, free activity to become whatever they will be.

These ideas, found in Ficino[10] and his predecessors, were presented by Pico with a special emphasis on the significance of freedom. In a brief but elegant and moving *Oration,* this young but learned son of an Italian count left us one of the most inspiring Western visions of humanity.[11] Pico shared with his teachers and contemporaries a view of humans as rational, highly intelligent, keen of sense, and, indeed, but "a little lower than the angels." The truly distinguishing human feature, however, is something else—an "indeterminate form" that can be given shape only by its own decision and doing. God had "animated the celestial globes with eternal souls; he had filled with a diverse throng of animals the cast-off and residual parts of the lower world." Having filled up everything, the creator then, desirous of having someone to study and love and wonder at this great work, decided to make man. But since there was nothing left from which this new creature could be fashioned, God decided to take the qualities of all the archetypes and combine them as a bundle of potentialities that would be at Adam's disposal to make of them what he would. Then God said: "We have given to thee, Adam, no fixed seat, no form of thy very own, no gift peculiarly thine, that thou mayst feel as thine own, have as thine own, possess as thine own the seat, the form, the gifts which thou thyself shalt desire." Here is a different version of Genesis, here the preeminent "open" image of human nature.

As he filled out his myth, Pico made the distinction between humans and other creatures consist in this fact, that while brutes are "confined within the laws" made by God, no such bounds exist for Adam, who "wilt fix limits of nature" for himself and be "the molder and maker" of himself. Humans also differ in this way from the highest spirits, who, like animals, have their identities fixed by creation. Freedom, however, means that humans can make themselves brutes just as well as they can grow into higher divine natures. It also means that the process is not one of making just anything at all out of nothing; humans have within them "every sort of seed and sprouts of every kind of life." But potentiality here is not the sort that manifests itself in a natural or determined unfolding. The various seeds require cultivation, and only those will grow that are cultivated through human exertion. "Who," Pico asks, "does not wonder at this chameleon which we are? Or who at all feels more wonder at anything else whatsoever?"

Pico's insistence on human freedom to make of humans what they *will* seems clear enough. It is through the "liberality of the Father" that "we make the free choice, which he gave to us," to help or harm ourselves on the way to salvation. Yet, as Kristeller observes, it is unlikely that Pico had abandoned the idea of grace. When God addresses Adam in Pico's myth, it is before the Fall. And when it comes to a matter of actually reaching oneness with God it is clear that Pico would agree with Ficino that this is a thing of such difficulty that it can be achieved only in another life. Pico's belief that we have within us a potentiality for brutishness as well as divinity is more strongly stated in the *Heptaplus,* where he notes how closely lust and anger accompany the cognitive powers of the soul: "the brutes are within our bowels, so that we do not have to travel far to pass into them." The "first Adam," a victim of Satan, can become the "newest Adam" only by grace, and our regeneration in this fashion will be "not as men but as adopted sons of God."[12]

These are serious theological points. Yet it should be possible today to read Pico's celebration of freedom without benefit of theology and as an independent myth about human dignity with stirring implications for human thought and action. If anticipations of Pico's views can be discerned in earlier Christian writings, and if it is difficult to reconcile parts of the *Oration* with Pico's own Christian outlook, the stark difference between his and Augustine's conception of what it means to be a human being is inescapable.[13]

Theological complications of the Renaissance humanist image of human dignity were largely avoided in Giovanni Gelli's *Circe*.[14] In this delightful series of dialogues between Ulysses and the Greeks transformed into animals by the enchantress Circe, Pico's vision is conveyed by the old stratagem of comparing humans and beasts. Circe, having promised to restore the Greeks to human form only on condition that they agree to the change, is amused by Ulysses' failure to convince one animal after another to be human again. The animals argue essentially that it is easier to be an oyster or a hare or a dog because nature provides not only their basic material needs but also a set of behavior patterns that make decision making or choosing unnecessary and virtue irrelevant. The horse recalls that as a man he had not often done what really befits manhood, but as a horse he has achieved the perfection of his kind with no effort at all. Ulysses' arguments about the refinements of human life and the superiority of human understanding or intellect carry little weight against rejoinders concerning the dire results of people's incontinent indulgence in luxury and the absurdities into which they have been led by their finely honed but tortuous reasoning.

As the dialogues proceed and one animal (the elephant) is eventually persuaded to resume human form, Ulysses must finally come to the point that it is precisely the difficulty of being human that makes human life worthwhile. Human freedom makes it hard to be a human being. Where an animal is led by its senses and appetites to pursue the convenient and shun the inconvenient, a person "wills or declines freely that which by his intellect he judges to be good or evil."[15] And this freedom of will and power of intellect by no means guarantee good choices. Gelli reiterates the common Renaissance belief that human nature allows for both good and evil actions, and notes again how individual effort is required for an expression of either of these possibilities. Nor is the intellect infallible in its determination of the good; error is possible, indeed easy. This is not to say, however, that good and evil are *in* human nature as productive forces of good and evil acts. Nor is it to say that reason is essentially error-producing. Human beings are free and willful in their moral and in their intellectual *activity*. Gelli then caps the argument by observing that human beings not only possess freedom of will and power of intellect—they *know* they have this freedom and power; they are *conscious* of it, "Upon which account, man only, of all other creatures, can know his own excellence." [16]

Human nature as an *entity* is denied from this Renaissance perspective. The Aristotelian belief in a nature for each thing comprising its causes and essential properties becomes inapplicable to humans. Man is not, by nature, a political animal in the sense that he is destined by his constitution to realize himself ultimately in the *polis*. Nor is he any other such kind of potential that will unfold in its predetermined way.

This Renaissance view of humanity runs strongly counter to ancient and medieval habits of thought that called for an understandable arrangement of all beings in a hierarchy of existence, with specific identifying attributes for each member. Denial of an ontology of human nature in favor of viewing humans as "coming to be" also failed to address the accepted problem of being and becoming. And the freedom that the humanists gave to the human will seemed to ignore as well the necessity inherent in the Aristotelian conception of *phusis* and in the emerging scientific idea of nature soon to be formalized by Descartes.[17] Finally, it was difficult to reconcile the disordered scene implied by an enfranchised and powerful human will with a belief in a single omnipotent and omnipresent God whose attention and control extended even to every detail of the human drama. It was in the context of this last problem that the myth of human freedom was reformed by Christian theologians.

[3]

Particular ideas about human nature are not, of course, formed and expressed merely as reactions to other ideas. The sixteenth century's strong assertion of human impotence was much more than a confirmation of an old deduction from divine omnipotence. Europeans at this time launched repeated and unprecedented attacks on human dignity, shaping a negative image of humankind that has survived to the present time as a "realistic" picture of men and women in their everyday conduct.

What might have occasioned a return to Augustine's darkest portrayal of the human being has been a subject of much historical research. Theodore Spencer [18] points out that the traditional Christian exposition of human wickedness and weakness had come to be supplemented by even more serious convictions about human insignificance. Sinful though they were, humans had still been regarded by the divines as God's central concern. But the awful implications of the Copernican revelation were beginning to dawn. God had become the creator of an infinity now more real and boundless, a universe in which humans occupied a nutshell amidst numberless other domains containing who-knew-what other creature products of God's limitless power. The human being had become "a tiny speck on a third-rate planet revolving about a tenth rate sun drifting in an endless cosmic ocean." [19] It was difficult, after Copernicus, to believe that God would give undivided attention to Adam's progeny. At about the same time Machiavelli pointed to the chaotic political scene for a clear warning of human incapacity for orderly social life. And then Montaigne summed up the gathering counter-Renaissance [20] claim that humans were not entitled to a distinct place in the order of nature; they were no different from other animals. Thus European consciousness of and security in a cosmic, a political, and a natural order were threatened by new secular outlooks.

While the collapse of conceptual cosmic and natural orders might put in question the possibility of a comprehensible social or political order, by the sixteenth century there were more tangible signs of actual social chaos to engender anxiety. Crisis had been precipitated by the breakdown of a medieval social structure of hierarchies, roles, and networks of obligation. Social disruption was aggravated by the troubled emergence of a new political economy and replacement of local and personal bonds of allegiance by the complicated and cold machinery of a distant yet pervasive sovereign state. Dislocations occasioned by such radical changes in social organization left people uncertain about rules in their lives. Gone was the conviction that a natural order in society, discernible to human reason, must eventually prevail. As William Bouwsma has recently shown with convincing evidence, a figure like John Calvin (1509–64) would look anxiously upon the disordered scene and be convinced that men and women had fallen to new depths of sin, where they lay helpless and in grave danger of completely losing touch with their creator.[21]

Martin Luther (1483–1546) earlier made this central point in the Reformers' case: humans are totally incapable of dealing with the mess into which their sin has led them. That the church had failed them in their time of distress was recognized as an immediate problem, but the ultimate source of human troubles was seen to lie in humans themselves. They had no one but themselves to blame. It was folly, therefore, to suppose that these helpless creatures could exert themselves effectively to change their lives. No, far worse than folly, for a belief that people can choose and control their way of life was precisely the awful sin of pride that had produced their misery and anguish. They must relinquish any claim to a free will—"that wretched thing, free choice"—and deliver themselves entirely to God's will. This was Luther's message of comfort: "even if it were possible, I should not wish to have free choice given to me, or to have anything left in my own hands by which I might strive toward salvation. For, on the one hand, I should be unable to stand firm and keep hold of it amid so many adversities and perils and so many assaults of demons, seeing that even one demon is mightier than all men, and no man at all could be saved; and on the other hand, even if there were no perils or adversities or demons, I should nevertheless have to labor under perpetual uncertainty and to fight as one beating the air."[22] For Luther, to deny humans free will is only to deny them divinity, and since *all* power belongs to God, *no* power belongs to humans. In the Reformers' revival of Augustine this basic view of God's omnipotence had far-reaching implications for human impotence and bondage. The details were worked out by John Calvin.[23]

The notion of *inherent* qualities is a basic feature of Calvin's doctrine of human nature. He speaks not just of how people act but of what makes them act that way. He does not generalize about human doings so much as he gives examples of human behavior that reveal forces within humanity as such, these forces having been identified in myths recounting the creation and tragic alteration of the first human, Adam. What Adam was as created and what Adam was after the Fall, and what all Adam's descendants have been were for Calvin ontological questions—matters of essential properties or propensities that have their origin and their explanation in the will of God.

How Adam's sin becomes our sin was apparently a troublesome question for Calvin. He argues that the transmission is not physical, although he refers to the "contagion" of sin, the "hereditary taint" contracted from Adam, and the "seed of sin" an infant carries from its mother's womb. Calvin cuts the discussion short, as he so often does on difficult points, by observing simply how "it had been so ordained by God" for both Adam and his descendants to lose the gifts bestowed upon them. The important thing, in any event, is that the "contagion" imparted by Adam "resides in us." It is a constituent and inescapable part of us.[24]

"Original sin" is the name given by Augustine and accepted by Calvin for this innate disposition to evil in humans. We sin "of necessity" because of promptings within us. It was very important for Calvin to deny any sort of external compulsion to sin. The denial extended even to ignorance as a fundamental source of sin. We *are* ignorant, and reason cannot reveal to us the basic laws of right conduct. Indwelling sin for Calvin is a positive and unalterable part of our nature. Humans are not merely bereft of Adam's original righteousness: "For our nature is not only destitute and empty of good, but so fertile and fruitful of every evil that it cannot be idle. Those who have said that original sin is 'concupiscence' have used an appropriate word, if only it be added . . . that whatever is in man, from the understanding to the will, from the soul even to the flesh, has been defiled and crammed with this concupiscence. Or, to put it more briefly, the whole man is of himself nothing but concupiscence."[25]

The necessity of human sin thus results, for Calvin, from our own lust, from a mind that is "a sink and living place for every sort of filth." Sin comes easily, on the slightest temptation, with no need for compelling external forces. It is not as if a capacity for evil is there to be used on occasions of provocation or of a temporary weakness of will. Calvin insists that the evil in our nature is an active force—"it cannot be idle." There is, indeed, no good to be found in us ("oil will sooner be pressed from a stone"), but to suppose evil to be merely the absence of good is to gravely underestimate human iniquity.[26]

It is true, Calvin conceded, that humans are not animals, for we have some conception of honesty, we are capable of some understanding (though not wisdom), and we have a limited awareness of divinity (though no real knowledge of God). Human beings are also social animals and their reason leads them to conceptions of justice and political order, although Calvin points out immediately that even in its struggles with such earthly matters the human mind "limps and staggers." The image of God in humans was not, then, entirely obliterated with the Fall. Yet, Calvin's final judgment is severe. Adam's sin resulted in corruption of our natural endowments and a total loss of our means to salvation. The "undoubted truth" of Augustine's sense of the human condition must stand: "the mind of man has been so completely estranged from God's righteousness that it conceives, desires, and undertakes, only that which is impious, perverted, foul, impure and infamous. The heart is so steeped in the poison of sin, that it can breathe out nothing but a loathesome stench."[27]

Calvin's reiterated assertion of an "inner perversity" in human nature is used to drive home the point that we are not only helpless in the presence of our compulsive wickedness but our denial of the compulsion is an integral part of the wickedness. Any claim to virtue is itself a sin. So, too, any claim to strength is a sign of weakness, for he who claims to understand God's mysteries "is all the more blind because he does not recognize his own blindness." Both the denial and the claim are taken as signs of pride. Then, as a clincher to his argument, Calvin asserts that people denying their depravity and claiming goodness not only sin in doing so but reveal their weakness in this self-deception. Hypocrisy is thus evidence of both evil and impotence. We are not even conscious of our selfish motivations, and any denial of them testifies to their reality. For "if some men occasionally make a show of good, their minds nevertheless ever remain enveloped in hypocrisy and deceitful craft, and their hearts bound by inner perversity." Seeming virtue is actually sin, therefore, and a display of beneficence to others is really selfishness. And people can carry on this sham with no consciousness of doing so, "for the natural man refuses to be led to recognize the diseases of his lust," and even philosophers attend only to the grosser images of lust and ignore "the evil desires that gently tickle the mind." Calvin found it difficult to discover for himself the secret springs of human behavior and almost impossible to convince other humans about their real motives because "the human heart has so many crannies where vanity hides, so many holes where falsehood lurks, is so decked out with deceiving hypocrisy, that it often dupes itself."[28]

Given Calvin's general disparagement of human intellect, and especially of human insight into God's works, the familiar question arises as to how this man, Calvin, could come to know in such detail what God had put into Adam and had then altered in Adam and all his descendants. Calvin himself gave the matter little attention beyond claiming to rely on scriptural testimony instead of reason when seeking spiritual discernment.[29] Interpretation of scripture raises more problems, however, and when we come down to cases it is clear that Calvin's myth of human nature is Augustine's myth presented in somewhat darker colors. We are left with the same difficult questions raised about the sources of the Augustinian version, and no more satisfactory answers are apparent. Bouwsma's argument that Calvin's depiction of human sin and weakness reflects his deep anxiety about the destiny of Europeans in an age of uncertainty is persuasive. When affairs seem to have been taken out of people's hands a confession of guilt and helplessness can be regarded as not only realistic but also comforting when accompanied by faith in external powers, whether those be divine or natural. It should be clear, in any event, that Calvin's "realism" does not rest on any sort of empirical base. His image of human nature was concocted, at best, to make sense of a situation of turmoil and, at worst, to deliver people into the hands of authority.

When Calvin focused on inherent properties of human nature he concerned himself chiefly with what people should feel guilty about —their constitutional depravity. Powerlessness is the other major quality he put into human nature. The two aspects are closely related in the human make-up as Calvin describes it, but the form of his argument for human weakness is more clear-cut and convincing. Christian theology concerning evil is plagued with inconsistencies not only about bad things flowing from a good God, but about the persistence of bad news following the good news spread by quite extraordinary means. An impression of human weakness, however, was both in keeping with the confused situation of sixteenth-century Europeans and a logical derivative from belief in one omnipotent God. Calvin's case for human impotence was built on a detailed exposition of divine omnipotence, and it was made at a time when many people were ready to relinquish control of their lives.

Minor details emphasize the absoluteness of God's presence and power. For Calvin, providence produces every single thing in all its particulars—"even to the least sparrow"; "Not one drop of rain falls without God's sure command." It is by God's will that one baby is fed liberally and another meagerly, as witnessed by the fact that "some mothers have full and abundant breasts, but others are almost dry." There are no fortuitous happenings, no chance; "all events are governed by God's secret plan."[30]

But it is especially in human affairs, the doings of people, that providence brings all things to pass. God's providence can, it is true, work through an intermediary, but it can also work without an intermediary and even *contrary* to any intermediary. For the "plans and intentions of men" are themselves governed by God.[31] The total comprehensiveness of God's will means, for Calvin, that we would be mistaken to view the result of any human act as a product of human will. We must not, then, be confused by evidence of someone's intention or desire being fulfilled by means of his or her own acts. Such evidence of "outward success" has no bearing on the question of free will, which would have to consist in an inner "choice of judgment and inclination of will."[32] Again and again Calvin makes the ultimate point of the incompatibility of any such freedom with God's absolute power. If we give people power to shape their own ends, "where," he asks, "will that omnipotence of God be whereby he regulates all things according to his secret plan, which depends solely upon itself?"[33] Calvin's lone concession to human freedom is his mocking reference to that "slight thing," the freedom to do evil.[34]

Calvin had to deal with a number of difficulties raised by the concepts of an omnipotent and omnipresent God and a completely depraved and helpless human being. The earlier problem of how an inevitable sinner can be expected or admonished not to sin is accompanied by the more positive difficulty of how an utterly helpless being can be urged to seek a God who is almost wholly beyond its feeble comprehension. Calvin offers very little practical guidance to people he has confronted with this dilemma. In an otherwise moving and warm chapter on the need for and benefits of prayer he has to remind us how, as we address God, we must neither think that we are not sinners nor not think that we are sinners; and "fear itself" is enough to teach the need for constant prayer.[35]

Salvation comes from grace alone, not from any act of human will. The "very evil doctrine of Pelagius," who put the cause of salvation in a person's merit, must be rejected. Even those who choose to come to God do so by God's will, not their own; any contrary notion signifies the sin of pride. You are not "compelled" to sin, but you do sin "of necessity" simply because sin is in you. You succumb to Satan because the Lord does not "make you worthy to be guided by his Spirit." Why does he thus abandon you? That is not a proper question. It is in fact a sinful thing to suggest that God should have a reason for what he wills: "it is very wicked merely to investigate the causes of God's will." Your predestination to eternal damnation or salvation follows, of course, from God's omnipotence, and it is quite out of your hands. Salvation is in no sense a reward for good deeds. It is presumptuous for humans to think that they

can even "work in partnership" with God's grace. Why does God
not save everybody? Again, a bad question, for it is simply a matter
of God willing otherwise, and why he wills otherwise is his affair.[36]
Reason as it was known to the ancient world, to Aquinas, and to
the Renaissance Platonists and Aristotelians has no place in Calvin's
picture of divinity. It must yield to the inscrutable will of God, as
interpreted.

Calvin could not, and did not, of course, leave matters there.
When he called on people to "learn from Scripture what is pleasing
to God so that they may strive toward this under the Spirit's guidance" there was surely some suggestion of working in partnership.
When he said that God only sets "limits to our life," which he has entrusted to our own care, matters of baby food would seem to be our
responsibility and not left to unassisted providence. When he urged
us to take "counsel and caution, by which to comply with . . . providence," this must grant us some power of our own. Now a belief in
providence becomes more a comfort in distress, an encouragement
when effort is required and presumably effective, and less a real
explanation of human activity and its consequences. Now "second-
ary" and "inferior" become "human helps" in the practical conduct
of life.[37]

An attempt to weigh or to reconcile conflicting positions in Calvin's argument would appear to leave us finally with the fact that
his interpretation of divine omnipotence required him to represent
people as congenitally bereft of rational powers to comprehend the
meaning of their existence and constitutionally incapable of a social
and cultural life that would express much more than their innate aggression and lust. His contribution, like Pico's, has had a career and
influence of its own, independent of theological moorings and the
complications they involve. Not that Calvin's theology is a thing of
the past. It has served the Protestant cause well. About a third of the
Institutes, it should be noted, was devoted to the role of the church
in leading helpless souls into the society of Christ and keeping them
there.[38] Pick up such modern Protestant texts as Karl Barth's *Church
Dogmatics* or Reinhold Niebuhr's *Nature and Destiny of Man* and the
Calvinist portrait of people will be found there with all its essential

qualities intact. And, as Herschel Baker reminds us, there have been recent revivals of Calvinism in lay intellectual circles.[39]

[4]

The Reformation image of human nature is not, of course, an isolated theme of sixteenth-century theology. It is part of a strong general current of Renaissance doubt, pessimism, and disillusionment about what Hamlet would finally call "man . . . this quintessence of dust." John Calvin's concern about the jeopardy in which people stood and his conviction that severe measures had to be taken to protect human beings from themselves were widely shared in the sixteenth and seventeenth centuries. Machiavelli (1469–1527) had earlier seen the need for controlling these unruly and unscrupulous creatures by force and fraud and so advised his prince. Jean Bodin (1530–96) had a somewhat more tempered view of the political power required by the situation, but he did not doubt the need for an absolute sovereignty, and his recipe for its organization became standard in the creation of Western states. By the time Thomas Hobbes (1588–1679) drew an explicit picture of the human nature that necessitated Leviathan he was offering a traditional estimate of people and a now accepted political solution to the problem of social order. Degree and range of state power would be debated, but the need for political authority was generally granted. Calvin had not denied use of force to the church in its task of taming wayward humans, but a monopoly and more effective application of force were soon lodged in political organizations of unprecedented scope. Even as the struggle between church and state for the control of people's lives went on, however, there was little doubt, given the acknowledged debility and iniquity of men and women, that strong external restraint and direction were needed. Whether the decision to control followed from convictions about human nature, or an image of human nature was devised to justify controls that would serve certain interests, the myth of human weakness and depravity was now more strongly implanted in European thinking than it had ever been before. Meanwhile, besides the theological and political, there were literary and scientific contributions to the myth.

The most comprehensive, thorough, damning execration of Adam's breed appeared in Montaigne's *Apology for Raimond Sebond*. Taking the Christian theologians' humiliation of humans at face value, Montaigne (1533–92) proceeded to spell out what is left to humankind when each and every one of God's gifts to Adam is removed, countered, or perverted. The resulting picture would probably not have been denied by Calvin, but he might have reproached himself for lack of such inventiveness and zeal and style in mortifying his congregation. For Montaigne barred no holds in making people "bow the head and bite the dust under the authority and reverence of the divine majesty." He proposed to "crush and tread under foot human pride and arrogance," to expose "the inanity, the vanity and insignificance of man; to wrest out of their fists the miserable weapons of their reason." Humans, he argued, are generally indistinguishable from animals, and inferior in many respects. Not even our Christianity rescues us, for "there is no hostility that surpasses that of the Christian. Our zeal works wonders when it seconds our propensity to hatred, cruelty, ambition, avarice, detraction, rebellion. . . . Our religion was made for extirpating sins; it screens them, it fosters them, it provokes them." Montaigne concluded, with Seneca: "O what a mean and abject thing is man, if he does not rise above humanity."[40]

By the time of Robert Burton (1577–1640) there was little room for originality in the belittling of human beings. In his *Anatomy of Melancholy* (1621), however, there is a rising attention to the nastiness of people, a feature of human nature satire that Jonathan Swift depicted with greater art in the following century. Burton regarded love and hatred as the passions from which all others arise, and he took a very close look at love. Divine love, the love of a true Christian, would be a wonderful thing, but "egged on by our natural concupiscence" we are incapable of anything but a lust that produces hatred, violence, malice, torture, and "melancholy fits." What Burton called the "heroical" form of love between man and woman rages out of control and becomes "a furious disease of the mind." With Calvin, concupiscence usually remained somewhat abstract—forceful, to be sure, but almost mysterious. With Burton it became graphic and we get a fairly clear picture of how reason is overruled by passion, "the Soul is carried hood-winkt," and the understanding made "captive like a beast." It is not only "love-melancholy" that renders humans helpless, however; the heirs of Adam's sin are entirely depraved and weakened by the inescapable disease of ordinary love—a normal condition if it is to be judged by its pervasiveness.[41]

Calvin's thundering condemnation, Montaigne's insidious dissection, and Burton's wholesale pathology of human nature were succeeded in the seventeenth century by a variety of popular catalogs of human frailties, witty and pithy and generally shallow remarks or *maximes* peddled in Parisian salons. They are of interest now because they show us how ordinary and opportune and funny the libel of humans had become. La Rochefoucauld (1613–80) could speak of people's vanity, hypocrisy, deceit, malice, cowardice, vulgarity, violence, ferocity, and littleness of mind and hope to attract attention only by cleverness of phrase. Madame de Sévigné, we are told, could do no more than pretend to find his remarks shocking.[42] Bruyère (1645–96) no doubt voiced a commonly accepted judgment when he spoke of his own scathing remarks about men and women as simple descriptions of natural phenomena: "Let us not be angry with men when we see them cruel, ungrateful, unjust, proud, egotists, and forgetful of others; they are made so; it is their nature; we might just as well quarrel with a stone for falling to the ground, or with a fire when the flames ascend."[43] We had become quite a bit lower than the angels; it was only candor to admit it.

The blow struck by science was of a different kind and is not properly a part of the human nature mythology examined here. Copernicus and his successors had, indeed, provided ground for serious questions about the centrality and importance of humankind in God's vast creation. It was, however, a spreading conviction about the operation of universal and invariable laws of nature that was to have profound effects on beliefs about the efficacy of the human will. If Descartes left an opening for human intervention in the tight web of nature, Spinoza seemed to have closed it. Not only was human freedom to alter the natural pattern now in question; God's power seemed to have become irrelevant or unnecessary. An omnipotent nature, explicable by humans but still beyond their understanding, had taken the place of an omnipotent God whose unfathomable will produces all effects. The implied limitation on people's freedom and power to form and to comprehend the course and meaning of their lives was clear. And then as the methods and objectives of science were extended explicitly to social and cultural activity, with the aim of revealing nature's laws at work there as well, hard questions about human freedom and morality were unavoidable.

Enlightenment thinkers about human affairs had a troublesome heritage. They had to deal with an omnipotent God, a sovereign Leviathan, and the iron laws of Nature as they tried to construct a reasoned study of human social life and, at the same time, allow men and women freedom to act and ability to devise a rational morality of activity. The task proved difficult.

CHAPTER TWO

Shaftesbury and Mandeville

THERE ARE REASONS for expecting good opinions of human nature to be more common in the eighteenth than in the preceding two centuries of Western thought. "Enlightenment" implies a breakthrough in grasping a natural and a human order of things and a fulfillment of Francis Bacon's program for rational participation in that order. Confidence in the power and effectiveness of human reason and action could be expected to revive a vision of human dignity. Thus, although Enlightenment thinkers might not have formally abandoned the doctrine of original sin, it must have been clear to them that a belief in inherent and ineradicable human defect was incompatible with the vision of a world that could be seized and reshaped by rationally directed human effort. While God could still be recognized as the author of human being, the emphasis now was on humankind as a part of nature and, therefore, subject to the same kinds of comprehension and controls used in understanding and dealing with other natural phenomena.

The new optimism is understandable. Europeans were justifiably impressed by their technological and scientific accomplishments. As Alexander Pope observed, God had said "let Newton be," and "all was light." In the battle of the books, the Moderns had prevailed over the Ancients with persuasive arguments about the superiority of recent intellectual achievements, and the integrity of their position was enhanced when they made their point with a scientific demon-

stration of how the operation of constant natural laws made for inevitable progress. It was evident that fear of the dreadful sixteenth-
century sin of pride could not repress buoyant enthusiasm about the
future. Grace and providence could still be seen as necessary and
basic, at least in especially difficult situations, but there was little
question about the efficacy of human activity in itself. If human
beings were not invariably capable and inherently good, there could
be certitude—or at least high hope—that perfectibility through
education or a change of circumstances was always possible.

Traditional views about human nature and the consequent perils
of the human condition persisted, however, but now more often in
practical forms concerning the problems of social life engendered
by people's selfishness. The problem of social order as formulated
by Thomas Hobbes might be derived ultimately from the doctrine
of original sin, but the consequences of disorder were now conceived
more as loss of life and property than as alienation from God. It
was nevertheless still seen as a serious human predicament, and old
habits of seeking its causes as well as its remedies in human nature
itself did not disappear.

There is much equivocation in the Enlightenment about human
nature; it is difficult to trace consistent lines of thought not only
among various writers but often in the work of a single thinker. In-
congruities appear in judgments about the goodness or badness of
people, their benevolence or meanness, their selfishness or altruism, and their fitness or unfitness for social life. There is also much
disagreement or vagueness about human capacity for conscious,
purposeful activity in the conduct of their lives—capacity for self-
government in the larger sense of the term.

The question of human goodness and badness and the question about humans' ability to conduct their own lives are related,
of course. Nevertheless, we encounter in the eighteenth century an
interesting attempt—even by moral philosophers—to discern and
describe and recommend a course of social life while setting both
questions aside. Again, the philosophers did not consistently maintain the claim that human social life has nothing to do with moral
action, but the results of their efforts to do so have important impli-

cations both for later social life and the search for knowledge about that life.

Boundaries and issues in Enlightenment discourse on human nature and society can be identified by looking, in this chapter, at the quite different views of humankind presented by two early eighteenth-century writers, Shaftesbury and Mandeville. Reactions later in the century to the problems they posed will be considered in the next chapter.

[1]

Anthony Ashley Cooper, third Earl of Shaftesbury (1671–1713) presented the favorable image of human nature that seems appropriate to the Enlightenment outlook. Although his efforts have won him a reputation for practically unrivaled head-in-the-sand naiveté about human beings, his views were by no means singular or isolated. Classical celebration of human reason and its power to discover a basis for virtue in truth was still widely respected, and it had only recently enjoyed a limited but significant revival even within Puritan bastions of Calvinist theology. A learned group of Cambridge Platonists and latitudinarian preachers took another look, in the late seventeenth century, at some implications of the Calvinist doctrine of the Fall and predestination, and what they wrote and preached is like a breath of fresh air in the cloisters of Restoration sectarian disputation.

The Cambridge Platonists' essential quarrel was with those who disparaged the efficacy of the human spirit or mind or reason in human history. A case has been made for seeing their efforts as directed chiefly against the materialism and determinism of Thomas Hobbes,[1] but their specific rejection of Calvinist predestinarianism and the idea of total human depravity is clear. Thus, a major concern of Benjamin Whichcote (1609–83) was to rescue from slander the "height and excellence of human nature, viz., our reason." It is a grave error, he argued, to suppose any conflict between reason and religion, for it is through the mind and understanding of humans that they are "made capable of God and apprehensive of him." Only by their reasoning ability can people come to know God and know what is good. And Whichcote was concerned to represent this exercise of reason as something more than contemplation of divinity. Action is involved. "No man," he tells us, "is born to be idle in the world." While material things might be provided us by others, "mental endowment" and "habitual dispositions" must be our personal accomplishments, for "everybody is master of his own fortune under God" and "every man hath himself as he useth himself." Then, echoing Renaissance views, Whichcote observed that by virtue of this power humans can elevate themselves to converse with angels or sink to brutishness and "finally shrivel up, and come to nothing." Human capacity for reason is relevant to the whole question of evil and goodness, for when humans sin they offend themselves as well as God, since they have "within" themselves a "principle . . . of self-recovery."[2] A human being is not the hopeless and helpless creature that Calvin portrayed.

In addressing the question of free will, Ralph Cudworth (1617–88), perhaps the most scholarly of the Cambridge group, was concerned to recover for humankind an ability to map a course of virtuous conduct and to act consciously and effectively in its pursuit. There is "something in our own power," he insisted, to do the good that God rewards and to avoid the evil that he punishes. To assume otherwise—that we are passive objects determined by inevitable necessity—appeared to Cudworth to subvert the whole point of Christian teaching that we should do good. The Kantian argument was made explicitly by John Norris (1657–1711): "a creature void of liberty cannot be capable of law or obligation, virtue or vice, reward or punishment."[3]

Besides defending the rational capacity of humans, the Cambridge group insisted on natural human goodness. People are loving, gentle, fair, benevolent, and mutually helpful to one another, according to Whichcote. There is a dignity about our nature; we are made for "much more than the slavery of sin." It would be a mistake, however, to suppose that Whichcote and his fellow preachers were unaware of, or interested in denying, the existence of sin and sinners in their world. Their point was, rather, that sin is not characteristic of humans, it is not inherent; it is an unnatural condition found only in a "diseased" mind, a mind disfigured by the accidents and violence of circumstances. "Virtue," on the other hand, "is the health, true state, natural complexion of the soul."[4]

These arguments were pursued in detail by Shaftesbury, who was evidently an amiable man. How good or original a philosopher he was has been disputed, but he does appear to have supplied in his conduct and his writing a model for the "good-natured" man of eighteenth-century English literature.[5] Disgusted by the bedizened reflections of Montaigne's skepticism that had appeared in such writings as Rochefoucauld's *Maximes,* Shaftesbury undertook a thorough rehabilitation of men and women as moral subjects. For Shaftesbury the crude vulgarities about alleged human frailties represented not just a modish pose among disgruntled French aristocrats, but symptoms of a real threat to classical views of human dignity and worth. In religious doctrine he went so far in rejecting Calvinism and embracing Pelagian ideas of human goodness and freedom that he was suspected in some quarters of serious heterodoxy.

The good nature that Shaftesbury saw in humans was in many respects composed of the same qualities pointed out by the Cambridge Platonists. People are honest, just, benevolent, faithful, and virtuous. Shaftesbury made the telling rejoinder to Hobbes's contract theory: the promises made in the contract could be considered obligatory only upon an assumption of good faith among the parties, and since the pledge was made in a state of nature, then good faith must have been as characteristic of people then as now.[6] Hobbes erred in representing humans as absolutely selfish, for this is to oversimplify the genesis of human action. A more careful look will reveal that "passion, humour, caprice, zeal, faction and a thousand other springs, which are counter to self-interest" play a large part in human affairs. Attempts to reduce all virtue to selfishness are strained and misguided. Honesty, friendship, affection, magnanimity, and courage are all valuable and worthy in themselves, and not, as satirists had said, disguised self-love.[7]

Shaftesbury was engaged, however, in something more than

painting a rosy picture of human nature. Wrongdoing hardly escaped his attention, but, like the Cambridge philosophers, he attributed human iniquity not to inherent moral disabilities but to failures of reason in difficult situations. Mandeville's gin-soaked Londoners were well known to Shaftesbury, but he saw them as victims of social and cultural conditions that undermined, degraded, disturbed, and maimed their natural humanity. Like Rousseau later, he cautioned against mistaking the human consequence of a given kind of social existence for its cause. Evil in people was unnatural, even pathological, for Shaftesbury, but he knew that it did exist. He had misgivings, in fact, about "imposters" who "speak the best of human nature, that they may the easier abuse it."[8]

In a more positive sense, Shaftesbury's concern was focused on the central problem of moral order. As Ernest Tuveson has pointed out,[9] it is here that Shaftesbury goes beyond the latitudinarians by taking moral conduct as a part of the natural universal system of harmonies and order—part of the system studied by the new science. It is no longer merely a matter of defining morality as obedience to divine law, but of seeking a basis for a good life in the nature of human beings themselves. The "Order of the Moral World" had, he believed, been lost sight of amidst scientific preoccupation with the order of material nature; humans as moral beings had been left out: "You who are skilled in other fabrics and compositions, both of art and nature, have you considered of the fabric of the mind, the constitution of the soul, the connection and frame of all its passions and affections; to know accordingly the order and symmetry of the part, and how it either improves or suffers; what its force is when naturally preserved in its sound state, and what becomes of it when corrupted and abused?" We concern ourselves, he noted, with the balance of trade or of power in Europe, but we neglect the "balance of [our] passions" and fail to think of "holding these scales even." Shaftesbury, more than most of his contemporaries, felt a need to capture, or recapture, a rational vision of a moral order whose "beauty and decorum" would match that of the natural order.[10]

The morality and the immorality of humans were, for Shaftesbury, naturally acquired traits or qualities, not simply gifts of grace or products of inherited conditions. We are, it is true, endowed with sentiments or affections or passions that are the sources of goodness and virtue—of any moral action. But the balancing of these emotional movers (as between self-serving and altruistic actions, for example) and their guidance by reason, are matters that involve the active participation of people in making their moral selves. Self-realization and, in a sense, self-transcendence, must, Shaftesbury emphasized, be understood as social in context and substance. Virtue consists in doing good for others, vice in harming others, and only through social actions of this kind do we benefit or injure ourselves. Such moral conduct is not automatic, not a manifestation of an attribute of given persons, but a conscious, striven-for course of activity. Shaftesbury's good-natured man is not simply an affable person who likes to please, but one whose temperament, reason, and sound judgment lead to considered virtuous deeds in concrete social situations.[11]

People, then, are of course fit for social life with their fellows. They are prompted in this by strong sentiments of benevolence and sympathy, and they are guided by reason. Here was Shaftesbury's reply to Hobbes's problem of social order: the problem exists only on an assumption that people are moved by fear and selfishness alone. But Shaftesbury went beyond his case for human good nature in accounting for society. Human beings, he insisted, are always found in society; they cannot exist without society; sociability, too, is in their nature. Social life is preservative of humankind, necessary to its survival. How, he wondered, could anybody have been puzzled about the "invention" of society or civil government when the principle of association or "herding" is so strong in people that it has produced factions that have in themselves produced disorder in "the general society of mankind."[12] The Hobbesian image of "solitary" natural man is an illusion.

Beyond Shaftesbury's undeveloped idea that certain human attributes exist because they have survival value for the species, there is not much in his work or in the writings of the Cambridge Platonists that lends empirical support to their views of human nature. Resting on the proposition that a good God created humans, the Platonists drew the conclusion that humans must be inherently good. Shaftesbury went but little further in his argument that goodness in people is the foundation of society, which is necessary to human existence. In both cases, these men were taking a *moral* position, a position that humans must be of this nature, and must be regarded to be of this nature, if what they thought of as a Christian way of life was to be possible. They constructed a myth of human nature to serve that purpose.

[2]

When Bernard Mandeville (1670–1733) presented his picture of human nature it is equally plain that he put into humans qualities that he could then point to as productive of certain outcomes he had predicted. One might approve of Shaftesbury's outcomes and disapprove of Mandeville's, but the fact remains that the evidence about human nature was minimal in both instances. Mandeville's candor about this makes his case more demonstrative of familiar patterns in human nature mythology. His procedure is a caricature of human nature theorizing, and he might have intended it to be so.[13] When he sought the origin or function of any practice or institution, he tells us, he did not bother himself about times when or places where but went directly to the fountainhead, human nature itself, and uncovered there the spring that produced the social phenomenon in question. And when he ran into difficulties along this path, he confesses, he simply had recourse to "conjectures" to make his way.[14]

Mandeville's depiction of human frailties was by no means novel. What he uncovered in human nature was quite different from what Shaftesbury had found, but it did not differ from what the Reformers and more recent Christian theologians had found. All human action and willing derive from self-interest and pride. Every virtuous deed is reducible to egoism. The pleasures sought by humans are material and sensual only. It is possible, Mandeville conceded, that virtue might prevail in small, poor, and rural societies, but not in the great cities of Europe.[15] In offering this tradi-

tional view of human nature, Mandeville correctly observed that
he was saying only what Montaigne had said before him[16] and (as
Montaigne had made clear) what Christian divines had long been
preaching. And, although it was only in passing, Mandeville did not
hesitate to attribute the low condition of mankind to the Fall as it
was conceived in Christian theology. The contents of human nature,
then, are already provided for him by generally accepted dogma.
His claim to have diligently perused the book of human nature[17] is
disingenuous. He would better have claimed to have read Augustine or Calvin.

Mandeville attracted attention, then, not with his familiar portrayal of human nature but with the disturbing manner in which
he represented human vice as the source of the wealth, the power,
and the civilized polish of societies like England. Shaftesbury had
it exactly backward: virtue could never have produced the good life
as that was generally understood. Greatness in nations rested on
foundations of selfishness, pride, gluttony, luxurious indulgence,
venality, and vanity. The paradox of private vices making for public
benefits is thus the centerpiece of Mandeville's tale. A notion that
good results can flow from evil intentions and deeds was, again,
not new with him (Vico had revived and used the idea at about the
same time), but the context and the striking manner of Mandeville's
presentation gave it unusual notoriety and so occasioned unusual
repercussions in a society that was at the time indulging in self-
admiration.

He made the point on several levels. Commentators like Kaye,
Hayek, and Horne[18] find support in Mandeville for the broad liberal
thesis that selfish pursuit of individual gain in the marketplace has
beneficent consequences in the form of meeting public needs and
desires. A colorful example is furnished in Mandeville's proposal for
the establishment of public houses of prostitution.[19] Demand in this
instance is met naturally by a supply created by the demand itself:
prostitutes are produced by seduction, which, of course, is only a
reflection of the demand for women who are, as Mandeville put it,
"comatable." The greater the need, the greater will be the supply, no
more, no less. Lecherous men who ruin innocent lasses do not have

the *intention* of keeping whorehouses well stocked in just the right numbers, but that is the convenient result of their self-indulgence.

At another level Mandeville gave abundant specific examples of ways in which vices produce wealth and comforts usually thought of as flowing only from beneficence and virtue. Indulgence in luxury is one of his favorite items. He acknowledged the Reformation's responsibility for a measure of England's prosperity, but he gave equal credit to the invention of "Hoop'd and Quilted Petticoats." The economy owed much to women's insatiable demand for finery, and it was to be noted how few wives "scruple to Employ the most tender Minutes of Wedlock to promote a sordid Interest."[20] Although gin might be seen correctly by guardians of morality as destructive of both health and upright conduct, its production and consumption contribute greatly to the employment of the poor and the wealth of the rich. In the case of the cheaper liquors, although we can recognize their dire effect on mind and body, we must also note that, besides their contribution to the public treasure, they can, with moderate use, ease the weariness and afflictions of the poor and uphold the courage of soldiers.[21] Thievery is no doubt evil, but we must grant that it keeps locksmiths in business.[22] Prostitution is railed against by the high-minded, yet if courtesans and strumpets were to be prosecuted with the rigor that silly people demand, would not the honor of wives and daughters be endangered? "Where six or seven Thousand Sailors arrive at once, as it often happens at *Amsterdam,* that have seen none but their own sex for many Months together, how is it to be suppos'd that honest Women should walk the Streets unmolested, if there were no Harlots to be had at reasonable Prices?"[23]

The larger implication is clear: Mandeville was reminding us that the consequences of human doing are not always anticipated by the actors, and that we must therefore be careful about interfering on misguided moral grounds. He warned that "the short-sighted Vulgar in the chain of causes seldom can see further than one Link; but those who can enlarge their View, and will give themselves the Leisure of gazing on the Prospect of concatented [*sic*] Events, may, in a hundred Places, see *Good* spring up and pullulate from *Evil,* as naturally as chickens do from Eggs."[24]

In such specifics about the function of a market economy and the indirect contributions of vices to material as well as immaterial gains, there was nothing very complicated in Mandeville's message, and he never pretended that there was. There was no mystery for him in the fact that a recognized evil, gin, made some people wealthy and other people temporarily happy or courageous. Larger implications for the wealth and power of a society were not as obvious, but generally at this level Mandeville was saying that people overlooked connections between evil and good because they were stupid or, more likely, because they did not want to acknowledge them.

Though Mandeville's depiction of human frailties was by no means novel, when he came to the larger question of the basis of order in human society, his argument became more serious and more sophisticated. Shaftesbury and others had maintained that people are sociable by nature, that innate sentiments of sympathy and benevolence, guided by reason, undergird a social order. Indeed, a human moral order guaranteed a human social order. Mandeville agreed that people are by nature sociable, but it is the evil in their make-up, he said, that produces society. Self-interest drives people into association with one another and keeps them there. In the beginning, Mandeville supposed, an interest in protecting themselves from animals leads humans into society; later they need it to protect themselves from other people. Also, they have an insatiable lust for material things that they cannot effectively indulge in isolation. But above all else, *pride*—that worst of all sins in the Christian catalog—drives men and women into a society of their fellows, for it is only there that they can seek and perhaps receive the approbation of others. In order, however, to satisfy our selfish desires for either material good or the approval of others, we must, as Mandeville saw it, conceal our selfishness from others. We must do this because pride is detested by all people, and the more so by the proudest.[25] Deceit and hypocrisy thus become the foundations of a civilized society. We pretend concern for others and we display benevolence toward others in order to secure the esteem of others and so nurture our self-esteem. Civility and politeness are outward signs of this concern, and people teach them to their children as soon as the value of hypocrisy becomes apparent.[26]

This abstract psychogenetic social history was accompanied in Mandeville's writings by what has been recognized as an anticipation of a developmental or evolutionary perspective. He repeatedly stressed the long span of human history, the finely graduated steps traversed in the formation of material cultural artifacts, and the slow unfolding of incremental phases in the emergence of habitual social behavior patterns. Although he never described broad stages of social evolution, there was a suggestion of trends or even teleological processes in human experience. All of this was still on a very general level, however, and is reminiscent of seventeenth-century speculation on the progress of knowledge. When Mandeville spoke specifically about such things as advances in ship construction, the persons involved in the process had no idea of or plan for the long-term results. Something was going on of which they were unaware.[27]

Mandeville was not content to leave matters there when he raised the question of just how a human passion comes to produce an orderly society. It could be argued that a strong emotion like pride would carry with it in people's make-up an awareness of need for an approving audience and hence the necessity of keeping society intact and functioning at any cost. Such direct and automatic psychogenesis of social order was not, apparently, satisfactory to Mandeville, for he introduces here another kind of deus ex machina to account for society—the mythical lawmakers or wise statesmen who manipulate people into believing that they should behave virtuously even though they are not naturally virtuous. This was not to be accomplished by mere admonition or by appeal to a nonexistent better nature in people; and Mandeville rejected the notion that religion might be serviceable here. The lawmakers turned, rather, to a frailty in human nature, pride. They flattered people by telling them how superior they are to animals, how sagacious and rational they are, and how they distinguish themselves as sublime creatures by subduing baser drives in their constitution. So-called innate moral virtues are thus revealed to be only "the Political offspring which Flattery begot upon Pride." (Mandeville shrewdly illustrated this process in microcosm by recalling to us how we heap praise upon children whenever they show any inclination to behave as we wish, and how the result is not only habitual behavior of the desired sort but genuine conviction on the part of the dupes that they act virtuously.) Finally, these wise shapers of human conduct are said to have completed the taming of savage natures by dividing all people into two classes, one that is told it has risen to the heights of moral conduct and another that is vilified as bestial. Thus emulation is introduced and a self-conscious group is persuaded to take a role as defenders of virtue against an ever-threatening crowd who would subvert the moral order.[28]

This conjectural history of the wise statesmen would seem to run counter to Mandeville's point about "concatented [*sic*] Events" and unanticipated consequences in human experience. Lawgivers and wily politicians, at least, appear to have known just what they were doing: public benefits have been derived from skillful management of private vices; the paradox is only apparent.[29] The elements of a plan here are so apparent as to suggest a parallel with Plato's outrageous proposal contained in the "royal lie." People are deceived into believing that they are something other than they really are, and so they are made fit for orderly social life. Mandeville's affront to human dignity can be regarded, in this narrow compass, as similar to Plato's: some people can know what they are doing, but most can know neither that nor what is being done to them.

The combination of myths about human nature and clever politicians did not convince Mandeville's contemporaries or successors that he had found a solution to the problem of social order. Perhaps this is because the work of the political manipulators in the scenario was so concrete that it called for historical verification, which was not forthcoming. If that part of the thesis merely served the purpose of dispensing with the notion of a social contract, it did not take one much further. For eighteenth-century thinkers the explanation of society had to be found in nature. Mandeville had chosen the passion of pride in human nature as a foundation, but the intervening actions of clever politicians complicated the story with historical detail. It smacked of personal intervention where natural forces or principles were required for explanation.

[3]

Later Enlightenment social philosophers could not share Shaftesbury's unreserved optimism about people and would not accept Mandeville's jeering. Shaftesbury's favorable picture ran counter to a long prevalent Christian image as well as to Hobbesian "realism." On the other hand, Mandeville's portrait of the human creature was so sullied by the unspeakable that moralists of the age would not take it seriously, at least in public. But there was a more basic problem. Shaftesbury and Mandeville had both engaged in a reductio ad absurdum of the whole argument from human nature. It was equally meaningless to try to solve the Hobbesian problem of social order either by asserting human goodness as a basis for peaceful social life or by postulating human badness as the foundation of social stability. Mandeville's case is more impressive, perhaps, because pride and selfishness are usually not expected to produce a working society, and he made a clever case for how they might. But neither man produced any evidence for the existence of their alleged traits of human nature or historical support for the actual manifestation of those traits in the foundation or maintenance of societies. Mandeville's importation of wily politicians to accomplish what he could not automatically derive from human nature indicates what might have been his own dissatisfaction with bare deductions from human nature mythology, but his politicians were also apocryphal.

That absence of real human beings—historical persons—in Mandeville's and Shaftesbury's conjectures makes them unconvincing. Real people doing things, planning and taking action, with observed results—all this is missing in their psychogenetic fantasies. The problem continued to plague their successors in Enlightenment social inquiry based upon human nature myths.

CHAPTER THREE

A Secular Idea of Providence

Thomas Hobbes had characterized people as unfit by nature for peaceful life in society and therefore in need of rigorous control by powerful political authority. Thinkers who wished to reject that analysis often thought they were confronted by the alternatives of finding a fitness for social life in humans, or of discovering an external source of social order other than Leviathan. Shaftesbury's good-natured man represents a rather simplistic version of the first solution. The second solution is suggested by Mandeville's account of how a thriving and smoothly functioning society is somehow produced unintentionally and unconsciously by the selfish behavior of Hobbesian people.

Other Enlightenment figures tried to combine more complicated forms of both of these approaches. When they looked for causes that could produce social results in ways beyond the control, the comprehension, and even the consciousness of people, they threatened to strip humankind of freedom to rationally design and act out a social life. But Enlightenment thinkers also undertook seriously to deny the operation of blind and unintelligible forces in human affairs and to endow human nature with ability and freedom to shape a rational moral order of social life. These were simultaneous eighteenth-century endeavors, and they were often combined in the work of a single author. A look at both ventures can reveal an interesting and influential episode in the history of human nature theory.

[1]

Precedents for seeking causes other than the purposeful acts of humans behind social and historical dynamics were common enough. Foremost among these was the idea of providence, a belief that God as creator and planner had ends in mind and used and directed people's endeavors so as to achieve purposes or goals unknown to them. A common feature of this line of thinking was to credit divine will with the power to employ human weakness and even iniquity in the achievement of good results. Mandeville's attempt to leave God out of this process occasioned outrage. In his magnificent *City of God,* Saint Augustine had created the prototypical example of finding in providence a productive force responsible for results that are preceded by tangles of seemingly discrete events. In his effort to give a rational account of the whole human drama, Augustine was faced with Scripture, which he could hardly ignore but which contained an apparent jumble of unconnected occurrences. He gave order and meaning to these by presenting them as episodes in the working out of God's plan to educate people in the ways of righteousness. What he needed for this operation was a knowledge of God—an intuition of what God had in mind—and while humility did not allow him complete access to the plan, Augustine managed enough to construct an account of lasting influence. The notion of a providence behind events, or of some variation on providence ordering the doings of humans, survived the Enlightenment.

But this notion survived only with difficulty and with suitable modification. Shaftesbury was clearly uneasy around the idea, although on one occasion he did remark how men who deny their benevolence and assert self-interest as their sole motivation fail to recognize how they can be "outwitted and imposed on by Nature, as to be made to serve her purposes rather than their own." [1] Mandeville, more adroit at keeping tongue in cheek, could abandon the reference to nature on occasion and account for good springing from evil by "the wonderful Direction of unsearchable Providence," and then in the same context attribute this accomplishment to "the dextrous Management of a skilful Politician."[2] In general, however, the concept of providence had proved so useful for so long that even when the new scientific outlook appeared to preclude reliance on it scholars looked for secular substitutes.

The difficulties, contradictions, and compromises involved in that search are perhaps nowhere better illustrated than in the work of Giambattista Vico (1668–1774) who, early in the eighteenth century, deliberately set about constructing what he called a "new science" of humanity. A central feature of the science was Vico's forceful affirmation that people create their societies, their histories, and themselves by their own activities. That, indeed, is what makes the new science possible, according to Vico, for it differs from the natural science that Descartes had talked about in that the subject matter of the new science is produced by humans and can therefore be understood by humans in a way that they can never understand the physical world, which was made by God. It would be difficult to make a stronger case for ruling out divine providence as an explanatory factor in human history, but Vico insisted nonetheless that providence has shaped that history. Why he took these seemingly contradictory positions has been a subject of prolonged debate among Vichian scholars, and it would appear that Isaiah Berlin was justified in observing that Vico offered no satisfactory resolution of the problem. For those who want to read Vico and ignore the recurrent resort to providence, nothing much would seem to be lost. But the matter cannot be left there, as if a noncommital pious gesture might be the only thing involved. For that astute man was saying not just that the integrity of history and culture implied something more than chance or contingency in human experience; he observed repeatedly that basic institutions in human society had been produced by the acts of people who had no intention of creating such institutions and no consciousness of having done so. Later observers can understand, in the spirit of the new science, what went on, but actors in the drama do not. So when Vico declared that people always make their own history he did not mean that they always know what they are doing. He could see no other way, evidently, to account for what he took to be complex and very important consequences of human acts that had no causal relationship to the plans or intentions of the actors.[3]

Although Vico had no apparent influence on later eighteenth-century social theory, the pattern of his thinking about unintended or unexpected consequences of human doing was common among Enlightenment thinkers. This is evident at a very general level in the case of progress theorists. Europeans by now had accepted the idea that there had been and would continue to be inevitable intellectual, material, and social progress but their optimism was characteristically tempered by a conviction that advance occurs only in the face of serious obstacles. While these barriers were often presented only as contingencies or accidents—wars, plagues, bad rulers, and so forth—more basic and abiding impediments were located in human nature itself.

Turgot, for example, expressed a typical counter-Enlightenment view when he observed that historical advance flows much more from the passions and blind strivings of people than from their reason. While rational control might prevail in the future, past progress actually was built largely on error and folly and certainly did not result from any human plan.[4] Condorcet, perhaps the most optimistic prophet of progress and the eventual triumph of reason, nevertheless presented a history of the human mind marked by superstition, blunders, and botchery resulting from natural human indolence and aversion to the new.[5] D'Alembert saw barbarism as the "natural element" of humankind; Jeremy Bentham admitted that the baleful influence of the "sad and mischievous passions" could never be eliminated in even the best ordered society; and Adam Ferguson saw man as "continually wedded to his errors."[6]

Auguste Comte, who so thoroughly summarized eighteenth-century social thought and laid foundations for modern social science, emphasized this fact that progress had taken place despite human errors and because of human errors. In an 1822 essay he explained the apparent paradox by attributing power to a natural law of progress, a law of the human organization itself. Any other accounting, he noted significantly, would have to involve "direct continuous supernatural guidance." And Comte was not engaging in far-fetched analogy when he went on to liken the situation to one in which a patient is cured when the physician's remedy is clearly wrong: "Frequent cures, effected in spite of a treatment manifestly erroneous, have revealed to physicians the powerful action by which every living body spontaneously tends to rectify accidental derangement of its organization."[7]

These attributions of effective agency to principles or laws of progress even in the face of human counteraction herald clearly a disposition to find an accounting for outcomes of social action in something other than the plans or intentions of people. But the abstract character of the discussion was soon to be modified by attention to more specific ways in which human pursuit of one set of objectives can produce quite different results. Development of this line of inquiry would do more injury to a belief in human dignity than had earlier vague allusions to the operations of providence or natural law.

Immanuel Kant (1724–1804) might be taken here as a transitional case. Although he did not go into anything like the detail of some of his contemporaries, Kant did seek, in his remarkable sketch for a universal history, to explain *how* it is that "unlovely qualities" and "egoistic pretensions" in humans lead us from barbarism to culture and from an asocial state to a lawful social order. The frame of his argument is like Mandeville's, but Kant's emphasis is on how all the latent creative forces in humans are activated by the resistance people meet in their mutual pursuit of self-interest. There is only a faint suggestion of paradox in this and more of a practical psychological consideration of requisites for human activity. The outcome, too, is not Mandeville's admittedly sordid hive, but a realization of human potential. Kant was saying, nonetheless, that humans have been moved by an innate propensity to action productive of consequences they did not anticipate, and his reference to both a "plan of nature" and "providence" in this context serves a purpose.[8]

When we turn to the works of the eighteenth-century Scottish moralists we find much more attention to the details of processes in which social results come to be through the disparate acts of individuals who did not intend to bring about those results. The Scots agreed that humans are moved basically by considerations of self-interest; Hobbes and Mandeville had been right, up to a point. But the threat to social order that this implied could not be met, as the moral philosophers saw it, by either force or fraud. Nor could it be addressed by Shaftesbury's bland appeals to a moral order flowing from sociableness or altruism or sympathy in human nature. More complicated mechanisms were conceived to this end, and as complexity increased, the social life of people came to involve something much more than the rationally directed activity of human beings.

This is not to say that moralists such as Adam Ferguson, Adam Smith, or David Hume took a generally unfavorable view of human nature. The optimistic estimate of humans that we would expect of the Enlightenment was indeed common. Hume chided those, like Mandeville, who would reduce every generous human act to selfish indulgence,[9] and there was agreement that people have strong social capacities. The passions or emotions that the Scots identified as sources of sociability were not as specific, as detailed, or as powerful as Shaftesbury's list, but they were sufficient foundation for a social order that might be built, as it were, inadvertently, by the actions of persons who did not have that particular end in mind.

This general stance was in keeping with Shaftesbury's refusal to find the sources of sociability in reason. Identification of the Enlightenment as an age of reason must be tempered with recognition of the strong emphasis that was placed by most thinkers of the period on the power and pervasiveness of the passions. Hume's famous dictum that reason is the servant of the passions[10] only exaggerates a prevalent conviction that while reason might be enlisted in guiding the passions down nonviolent paths, it must not be forgotten that emotions, drives, and propensities are really what makes the world go. Alexander Pope made the point nicely: "On life's vast ocean diversely we sail, / Reason the card, but passion is the gale."[11]

If, then, some social outcomes of human activity are not to be traced to rational plans, if a structure of social order is not to be found entirely in a rational order, and if we are to seek the bases of society rather in a human nature driven by self-interest, how do we avoid Hobbes's war of all against all? In part, of course, the

Scots' reply was simply that reason does guide and control individual drives for self-satisfaction in such a way as to curb violent pursuit of one's aims and to promote peaceful interaction. Thus Pope, again: "Two principles in human nature reign; / Self-love, to urge, and Reason, to restrain." [12]

But the matter was not left there, for when passion is given such power and reason is all but left out of the reckoning of what ultimately moves people, the Hobbesian device of suddenly calling on reason to prevail by revealing the long-range advantages of social life is hardly convincing. In place of—or in addition to—this solution to the problem, there was recourse to demonstrating how human social actions can have regular, natural outcomes unrelated to the intentions of the actors, whether those intentions be self-aggrandizement or altruism or any other aim. And given reigning scientific standards, the demonstration could not rest with literary paradox or with empty allusion to inscrutable providence.

David Hume provides a good introduction to the procedure. With his usual scrupulous attention to detail, he noticed how laws of justice arise from natural principles in a manner "oblique and artificial," for though rules of property, for example, contribute to the public good they arise from self-love. It is in the interest of each individual to be secure in his or her property, but since the selfish pursuits of each person must run counter to those of another, the several "interested passions" must be systematically adjusted. The resulting system is advantageous to the public, "tho' it was not intended for that purpose by the inventors." [13] Again, a "passion for public good" in people might produce a powerful, secure, and industrious community, but Hume could not rely on that.

Rather, other passions such as avarice and indulgence in luxury must be encouraged in order to move people to work hard to get the things they really want. This indirect approach to creating an efficient labor supply, Hume argued, will actually be the more effective way of making unneeded laborers available as soldiers; and people consuming luxuries will thus unintentionally be contributing to the security of the community.[14] In another context Hume had recourse to what Lovejoy has called the "method of counterpoise" to produce unintended public benefits from pursuit of private interest by knaves. This may be accomplished by checking one private interest by another through a division of power among different groups, for if a single faction is allowed unchecked power, only the interest of that faction and not the "public" interest will be served. The point, once more, is that knaves who vigorously work for their own aggrandizement are unwittingly working for the public good.[15]

It should be noticed—and quite appropriately in the case of Hume—that the unintendedness of consequences in social action often does not hold for all of the actors. Thus, in Hume's example of property law neither the lawmakers nor those who acted under the law intended the public outcome; but he made it clear enough that somebody "animates" people with the spirit of avarice and luxury and that a good "plan" makes for mixed government. Clearly those who animate and plan must intend the results they might so achieve. This equivocality, we have seen, was apparent in Mandeville, who could talk of providence and the manipulations of skillful politicians in almost the same breath. We can bear in mind, however, that in either case most of the people involved are represented as not knowing important social consequences of what they do.

Hume is also a good introduction to the other Scottish philosophers in his utilitarian rejection of motive as the key element in moral action. Where Mandeville had identified vice as anything that did not flow from disinterested motives—anything produced by egoism—Hume sought to reinstate self-interest as a virtue insofar as it promotes acts leading to public good. The consequences of deeds are to be the evidence for their goodness and badness, and whether or not the consequences are intended by the doer is irrelevant. The Scots generally followed this utilitarian principle.[16]

With Adam Smith this disregard for motive is carried to the point of actual distrust of good intentions. We should not, he wrote, look to the benevolence of the butcher, the brewer, or the baker for our dinner, but to their regard for their own interest; not to their humanity, but to their self-love. Moreover, we should actually be wary of benevolence. "Nobody but a beggar," he tells us, "chooses to depend chiefly upon the benevolence of his fellow-citizens,"[17] and "I have never known much good done by those who affected to trade for the public good." Intention to promote the interest of society is a less reliable means to that end than is the pursuit of self-interest. An individual who "intends only his own gain" is led "by an invisible hand" to further the public interest.[18]

Smith's conception of a social system at work for the accomplishments of ends unintended, and even opposed, by human beings became especially evident when he was concerned with human interference in the system. There are "speculative" physicians, he noted, who busy themselves prescribing detailed programs of diet and exercise, unaware that the human body "contains in itself some unknown principle of preservation" that in its own way works not only to maintain natural health but even to counter the bad effects of misguided therapy. The lesson of this wisdom-of-the-body analogy is clear: although the "folly and injustice of man" will on occasion create political economies that endanger the wealth of nations, there is a "wisdom of nature" to counter this effect through the "natural effort which every man is continually making to better his own condition."[19]

The language of providence was often used by the Scots when they referred to nonhuman sources such as an invisible hand to explain unintended results of human acts,[20] but this was largely window-dressing and should not obscure the natural character of the explanations sought. The Scottish philosophers were not simply attributing given sets of results to God and letting it go at that. They were looking for mechanisms in a system in which things came to pass by a now quite secularized providence.

Thus, Thomas Reid pointed out that humans often acted out of instinct or habit, without deliberation or will, in matters necessary to their well-being, their very existence, and the preservation of their communities. As a notable example (a favorite among the Scots) Reid offered the sexual urge, an inferior principle of action placed in us by the "Author of our being" to assure propagation of the species without relying on anything like human foresight. Similarly, we are prodded to activity by an innate susceptibility to unpleasant feelings occasioned by inactivity; to a search for power, knowledge, and esteem by strong desires for such things implanted by the Author; to peaceful coexistence with our fellows by "benevolent affections" bestowed by a wise creator. In all these instances reasonable deliberation plays no part, for although Reid sternly rejected Hume's claim that reason is only a servant of the passions, he acknowledged that reason is an imperfect guide to the achievement of many purposes. Reid's general orientation here is revealed by his comparison of many unintentional human acts to the complex activities of bees in their construction of honeycombs. God is said to be the knowledgeable actor or maker in these cases, but the actual mechanisms producing the results are instincts.[21]

Adam Ferguson is the clearest spokesperson for the Enlightenment in the matter of unintended consequences of human action. He makes the most of obvious cases: a powerful "mutual inclination of the sexes" conducts to the marriage institution; the wife-husband bond involves that of parent and child and the family organization; propagation is secured "without consulting the mind or the intention" of people—it is a thing that cannot be entrusted to the "precarious will" of humans.[22] How can anybody look at the "amazing fabric of language" without seeing in it something far above mere human ability?[23] In the larger matter of national progress or decline, political situation is the key, but that is sometimes shaped with "perfect blindness" to the future and ignorance of consequences. People would better themselves, but often "they know not whither" they drive.[24] The idea of a social contract was to Ferguson absurd, for relations of power and dependence arise naturally from circumstances of family, differences of strength, and leadership. Political refinements are designed on this basis, but people do not create society by compact.[25] Effects are sometimes produced before causes are known, the work often done before it is planned.[26] The productions of beavers, ants, and bees we know to be instinctive, but Ferguson saw the same basis in the establishments of humans. We project, he observed, but we cannot possibly know beforehand the complicated products, which are "the result of human action, but not the execution of any human design." The wise lawgiver and celebrated statesman of old are mythical figures (and Mandeville's clever politicians would no doubt fall into the same category). Humans, like other animals, proceed in "the track of their nature, without perceiving its end."[27]

[2]

These were serious attacks on human dignity, for much more than a simple assertion of people's depravity was involved. Enlightenment thinkers, while formally acknowledging the Fall, actually found much good in human nature. Calvin's incorrigibly sinful specimen gave way to a person who is naturally prepared for virtue and also intellectually capable of discovering and following a practical course of virtuous activity. But when it comes to life in civil society—to the conduct of public affairs, to action in a political economy—something like Calvin's lowly creature reappears, bereft of effective will, manipulated by an invisible hand, acting blindly to accomplish ends not its own.

All of this runs counter to a basic Enlightenment faith in reason and optimism about people's conscious control of their destiny. The contradiction might suggest inconsistency or equivocation, or simply that we must recognize the reality of a "counter-Enlightenment,"[28] but that is of little moment. More to the point is that we can find in some of the Enlightenment figures recognition of a problem here and a need for pressing the question of human power. It is in this undertaking that we discover a reaffirmation of human capacity.

Amidst his talk of providence and the apparently fateful course of history, Vico presented a carefully argued and eloquent case for human historical responsibility: it is in the minds of persons that the sources, controls, and ends of human activity are to be found. And we can know that and understand it in a way we can comprehend nothing else in nature. Vico provided what is probably the strongest intellectual defense against alienation in Western thought. For present purposes, however, more succinct and accessible expression of Vico's ideas can be found in the Scottish Enlightenment.

Part of the difficulty in handling the question of human control
of human affairs seems to have arisen in the reaction to Mandeville's
paradoxes. One way of meeting the paradox of "private vices, public benefits" was to deny that a good such as public benefits could
flow from an evil; the so-called vices, therefore, were not evil at all.
It is evident, however, that the Scottish moralists could not carry
that argument far. When Adam Smith invoked the invisible hand
to account for benefits to others flowing from the butcher's self-
interested acts it was, in part, because he was disturbed by the moral
problem of people apparently doing good without meaning to—unintentionally, indifferently. Smith did not need the invisible hand to
explain how we get our meat from the butcher; he immediately went
on to show how this resulted from the division of labor (which he
also accounted for in natural terms—a propensity to truck, barter,
and exchange). It is just as clear that he did not need the invisible
hand to explain how the poor benefit from indulgence in luxury by
the rich (which he again accounted for in natural terms—vanity).
And there is no good reason for supposing that the butcher and the
rich people do not know that their activities benefit others; indeed,
butchers and wealthy people are quick to say so and to lay claim to
virtue for so acting. Why, then, the invisible hand? For one thing,
to handle the problem of good arising from what Smith still regarded as "inferior principles of action." The traditional stratagem
of having a transcendent power use human frailties to accomplish
its ends is evident. Smith was not prepared to say that people acting
in the marketplace are free moral agents who intend by their acts
to benefit others. Still, he approved of what they were doing. So, he
said it was in their nature to do what they were doing, and what they
were doing was naturally explicable. The invisible hand seemed to
render amoral acts moral. It did not, of course, actually account for
the unintended consequences of human acts. There were, for Adam
Smith, economic phenomena that could not be explained as manifest consequences of human plans, but his objective was to find out
what human activities *could* explain those apparently "spontaneous"
phenomena.

His contemporary, Lord Monboddo, certainly could see no sense or moral stature in a doctrine that postulated hypothetical forces as explanations of the outcomes of human acts. What happens in human history, he declared, is not mere natural occurrence, which is produced by "inward principle." Human doing proceeds from "that impulse, moving the rational mind to action, which we call *will*." By our own powers we "make ourselves, as it were, over again," and all science, art, and society itself are products of rationally directed will. When Monboddo had to wonder how such a marvelous thing as language could have been produced by the human intellect, he would not resort to an invisible hand or other such force for explanation. He told what he could find out about the history of language and then candidly acknowledged that God might have taken a *direct* hand in the process. But Monboddo concerned himself only with the human "invention" of language.[29]

Considerations such as these might have led Thomas Reid to go beyond musings about instinctive and habitual activity and recognize the importance for "moral and accountable" creatures to know what actions are in their power, and to conclude "that man has power over his own actions and volitions . . . because he is capable of carrying on, wisely and prudently, a system of conduct, which he has before conceived in his mind, and resolved to prosecute."[30]

This was the essence of the moralists' position. A moral act must be a free act; moral conduct is intentional conduct. While Reid had recognized outcomes of human activities that are not willed or intended, it was will and intention and reasonable understanding that characterized human action as such. What action produces without intention can have no moral and, therefore, no distinctly human significance. Reid's belief that humans have the power to direct their lives rested ultimately on his belief in human accountability to God and to fellow humans. The bondage implied by any doctrine that places humans in a situation incomprehensible to them and beyond their power to control is incompatible with the life of moral agents.[31]

Reid's conviction that people can know what they are about involved rejection of both Calvin's general declaration of human impotence and David Hume's skepticism. We are, Reid argues, justified in acting, and we do act, on "probable" evidence. That is, we act on a presumption that our knowledge of how things have gone on in the past will be applicable to the present and future. A regularity that we have observed in affairs is a reliable basis for acting with an expectation that anticipated and intended results will follow.[32]

This belief in a natural order of things, comprehensible through rational inquiry, lies at the heart of Adam Ferguson's radical departure from his remarks on unintended consequences of human doing. Shaftesbury's reassertion of the traditional view of both a natural and moral order is echoed by Ferguson, but now with broad concern for its practical social implications. His argument is teleological: since humans are active creatures, the world must be governed by fixed laws: "If there were not any fixed connection of cause and effect, the wise could have no foresight nor practice any means for the attainment of an end." This means, of course, that the laws, though often complex, must be discernible to human beings, whose faculties make this possible and exist for this reason.[33]

It is clear that Ferguson was ready to recognize both intended and unintended consequences of human acts. Like so many of the Scots he was a great qualifier: in "many" or "some" instances, or "often" or "occasionally," ends are reached without deliberate consideration. When it came to major questions about historical progress, however, he was obviously uncomfortable with a view that something beyond the ken of the participants was taking place. So, nature will sometimes not entrust her work to a "subordinate agent": "But if the progress of man in every instance were matter of necessity or even of contingency, and no way dependent on his will, nor subjected to his command, we should conclude that this sovereign rank and responsibility of a moral agent with which he is vested, were given in vain." And this is not just a defense of moral agency, for Ferguson goes on to say that something like a science of human affairs is possible. If people can manipulate natural forces by virtue of their knowledge of natural laws, then they should be able to shape their own progress in the light of laws of human nature.[34] This is hardly the outlook of one who would regard the outcomes of human conduct as unrelated to conscious human effort.

Ferguson's estimate of the effectiveness of deliberate human activity rests on an image of human nature reminiscent of pre-Calvinist Renaissance opinion. Unlike mere animals, who remain unchanged in their nature, humans are not so bound, but are given freedom and intelligence to make themselves, for better or worse.[35] Humans, Ferguson said, are their own masters. By an exercise of will, by effort, they shape their conduct and they do so even along lines contrary to what instincts would dictate. In "some instances" they may behave as animals, but in "most instances" they act from design and in the light of knowledge that shapes ends and reveals means for their attainment.[36] In a discussion "Of Will and Freedom of Choice" Ferguson countered Luther's and Calvin's attack with the bold observation that humans not only have the power to choose among alternatives available to them, but they are *conscious* of that power, and they are conscious as well of the considerations on which their choices are based. Because the power of choosing is something of which the mind is conscious, no stronger proof of its reality is possible; for Ferguson, attempts to support the proposition by arguments are "nugatory" and attempts to deny it by arguments are "absurd."[37]

When Ferguson came to deal with economic institutions, then, he had at his disposal active and intelligent humans to comprehend and do things. There was little need to resort to transcendent forces or mysterious "engines." It is humans who learn "to distribute the tasks of men in society to suit the varieties of their disposition and genius." Different physical circumstances lead to surpluses and deficiencies of commodities in different places. Trade therefore arises, and this exchange, "though above the comprehension of any other animal, is perfectly obvious to man." Advances of the commercial arts can properly be left in the hands of self-interested individuals because the rich want to be rich and the poor want to escape poverty.[38] Not much need there for the invisible hand.

In his more general discussion of human nature it is evident that Ferguson was responding to the theological doctrine of original sin. He considers the problem of evil under two headings—the general circumstances of human life, and the depravity of human nature itself. The circumstances are harsh, he argues teleologically, because humans must, as active and learning beings, make choices between good and evil, and they must overcome trying conditions if they are not to sink into sloth. As to evil in human nature itself, Ferguson preferred to explain this as a result of "error and mistake" rather than seek any "deeper root," because error and mistake sufficiently account for the evil observed. He then rejected the notion that we are helpless in our corruption and dependent on rescue from without. "Moral discipline" will reduce evil, and human intelligence can discover a basis for the discipline.[39]

Reid, Monboddo, and Ferguson were not the only Scots who held such positive views of human nature, as a reading of Smith's *Theory of Moral Sentiments* alone must make clear. Still, the length to which Ferguson went in affirming the historical and moral powers of humans is unusual. It is as if a recoil from the idea that people act blindly in their social lives was strongest in the writer who had most clearly presented the idea, as if Ferguson was led to his celebration of human dignity by realizing the grave implications of his own notions that people are not responsible for their fate and are subject instead to forces beyond their awareness and control. In any event, the idea that people make their own histories and social and cultural lives is there as an alternative, alongside the idea that things come to be by the operation of forces and the effects of structures manifested in slow and tangled processes of change in which human beings only play roles written and directed by a source beyond their comprehension.

The Enlightenment offers us views of humans both as subjects who shape their society and as objects who are shaped by society. Both images are largely mythical, but which one we choose has significant consequences for how we seek to understand our social life and for how we conduct ourselves in that life. Modern choices between the alternatives show both the continuing strength of a closed image of human nature and the revival of a more open vision.

CHAPTER FOUR

Freud's Scientific Mythology

THE EIGHTEENTH CENTURY habit of taking an analysis of human nature as a point of departure in the study of society has not been characteristic of modern inquiry. Later efforts to enlist a scientific psychology in the construction of batteries of instincts for the identification and explanation of human behavior were generally recognized as futile enterprises and replaced by more direct approaches to social and cultural life. An obvious exception to this trend is the work of Sigmund Freud.

Freud's reflections on the dignity of human beings are noteworthy here for their striking re-creation and reinforcement of a traditional Western image of human nature. In both its construction and its substance—its derivation and its defining features—the Freudian portrait of humankind was essentially like the one drawn by John Calvin. It was mythical in source and depreciative in content.

[1]

The question of how Freud arrived at his knowledge of human beings involves at once the familiar puzzle of how anybody who begins by stripping the human intellect as such of rational power can claim to have arrived at real knowledge. Karl Marx tried to escape the burden of false consciousness by making his clear thinking a function of a particular social class position; but Marx did not brood much about epistemology. Calvin put himself in a more troublesome position by attributing his frailty to his biological descent from a tainted Adam; only by confessing his guilt, using the guidance of Scripture, and, perhaps, receiving a measure of grace could he claim to know anything about God or God's creation.

In Freud's case the problem was not simply a matter of having painted oneself into a corner from which some clever escape was needed. Freud was not saying, "Here is the truth, and you can believe it because here are my credentials." Freud started with establishing his credentials, and that establishment became the core of his doctrine. Psychoanalysis (in this unique instance, self-analysis) produced the fundamentals of psychoanalytic theory. It was in the situation of analysis that Freud revealed to himself the previously hidden structure of the human psyche.

In coming to know himself through self-analysis Freud claimed to know all other people and to know how to get such knowledge. Introspection had long been the name given to this procedure, but now Freud claimed to see things in himself that humans had not seen in themselves before. What made this possible? How do we test the results of the self-analysis, make them objective in any sense? These are difficult questions that should be kept in mind when Freud tells us he took a careful look at himself and therefore knows something about humankind.[1]

In his actual musing about himself and others, Freud was assisted by more than a probing honesty. No one in the history of human nature study has resorted more openly to myth for guidance. And his reliance on mythology was not limited to seeking hints or clues from the presumed insight or wisdom contained in folklore or in old stories about Oedipus or Narcissus and the like. As Wittgenstein noticed, Freud constructed a powerful mythology of his own, stories boldly made over or made to order when appropriate tales were not in the given supply.[2] He made no effort to disguise this procedure. He flaunted it, rather, as an appropriate part of scientific inquiry. So, he asked Albert Einstein, "does not every natural science lead ultimately to this—a sort of mythology?"[3]

In the matter of instincts ("at once the most important and the most obscure element of psychological research")[4] Freud was especially candid: "The theory of instincts is so to say our mythology. Instincts are mythical entities, magnificent in their indefiniteness. In our work we cannot for a moment disregard them, yet we are never sure that we are seeing them clearly."[5] The question of how one goes about "seeing" an instinct "clearly" was taken seriously by Freud, of course; he was aware of the demonstrated folly of merely positing an array of instincts to account for an order of acts. In the context of the above remark, therefore, he undertook to justify his vision of two classes of instincts, the sexual and the aggressive. His procedure reveals much about Freud's method of inquiry into human nature.

He began by saying that he would not rely here on historical or personal evidence of aggression or destruction in the behavior of people, but would turn instead to the "phenomena of sadism and masochism."[6] Having noted how sadistic and masochistic behavior in sexual relations involves satisfaction from inflicting or suffering pain, Freud said that this exemplified a mixture of sexual and aggressive instincts. He then supposed ("we proceed to the hypothesis") that every instinctual impulse is a similar mixture of the two classes of instincts. Masochism now becomes a sure sign of the existence of a self-destructive trend in people, and sadism is seen as the destructive instinct directed outward. But the possibility of our not being able to vent our aggression outwardly suggests that we will tend more to self-destruction, and so we are compelled to destroy other people (or things) if we are not to destroy ourselves. "A sad disclosure indeed for the moralist!"—Freud exclaimed in typical satisfaction with having shocked naive believers in human goodness.

The story does not end here, however. Just as he would not rely on historical or personal evidence for a destructive instinct, Freud now said he could not depict people generally as self-destructive "merely because a few poor fools have linked their sexual satisfaction to a peculiar condition." More profound consideration led Freud to see in the instincts an effort to "restore an earlier state of things," a "compulsion to repeat," a strongly "conservative" force. This he now identified as a universal natural process, and instances were suggested: the mucous membrane of the stomach digests itself; embryos repeat the phylogenetic process; many animals regenerate lost organs; fish return to spawn at their birthplace; birds repeat migratory patterns; and repressed childhood experiences are reproduced during psychoanalysis. But more: there is a fundamental process that works to do away with all life and to restore the inorganic state out of which it arose. The term "death instinct" suggests itself.

Freud observed at this point that he had merely reproduced Schopenhauer's philosophy, but had now confirmed it by "sober and painstaking detailed research." But research in the sense of discovering and using new facts in the formation and testing of conclusions, and then of considering possible alternate conclusions, is not evident in this set of assertions about a death instinct. Freud constructed a story here, an impressive tale of remote happenings and primordial conditions that might be taken to account for postulated qualities in human nature. The story (as Freud warned us) is not derived from observed occurrences.[7]

We are indebted to Freud for this effort to "see" an instinct in a manner that seemingly escapes the tautology of defining a force in terms of its effects and then explaining the effects by the force. It is one of the very few occasions in the literature on human nature when an author openly rules out all evidence from human experience as inadequate and seeks instead to derive an instinct from a series of abstract propositions about the nature of organic and inorganic matter in general. Freud's mastery of the technique and his powers of imagination and expression are impressive. But these are the tools of myth making, not of rational public inquiry. Speculations, hunches, guesses, and suppositions are all necessary parts of scientific work, but science does not begin and end there. On the basis of a few predilections and prejudgments deriving from his familiarity with masochistic behavior, Freud undertook to tell people that they are naturally bent on destroying themselves or, in lieu of that, destroying their fellows, and to represent that myth as a product of "sober and sustained research." Freud had no more evidence for such a sweeping proposition than Calvin had for his convictions about innate human sinfulness.[8]

Freud's reliance on myth for insight into human nature rested on a peculiar conception of the relationship of myth and truth, a conception that places the two not just on a continuum but renders them identical. A conjecture, a Just-So Story, a "scientific myth," and a hypothesis were the same thing to him.[9] His talks with patients, he told us, suggested to him that most children fall in love with one parent and hate the other; this was a hypothesis for him. He interpreted the Oedipus story as a tragedy based on a wish to love one parent and kill the other; he took this as a revelation of something very common if not universal in human experience—there is a "voice within us" that tells us that this is a real feature of human experience. Now the "validity" of the myth was taken by Freud to confirm the "validity" of the hypothesis about child psychology.[10] Myth was used to test a hypothesis.

The "voice within us," the "traces" left by experiences of the primal horde, and the meaning of dream symbols were, for Freud, lodged in the human unconscious and recoverable by the interpretation of stories, jokes, expressions, and myths. As Philip Rieff pointed out, the unconscious is Freud's "conceptual ultimate," something of which we cannot be directly aware but that we must assume.[11] Since the essence of human nature is revealed in the unconscious, knowledge of that nature is not, therefore, available through usual procedures of empirical science. Analysis can call up fragments of the unconscious, but only an analysis using myths for guidance and interpretation. And the myths must themselves be interpreted with guidance provided by what we know, indirectly, of the unconscious. The pitfalls of tautology, of circular reasoning, and of self-confirming hypotheses in these procedures are evident, and Rieff and others have represented Freud as well aware of such difficulties in psychoanalytic inquiry.

Freud was not always ready, however, to let evidence spoil a grand speculative structure. His insistence on the reality of inherited "memory-traces" that revealed primitive human experiences is a case in point. The events detailed in *Totem and Taboo* were said to have left traces in the unconscious of all humans, traces that are revealed by analysis. The questions was: How did those traces get there? Not, Freud said, by direct communication of any kind, but by "phylogenesis." They were, that is, acquired characters that had been inherited by succeeding generations. Freud knew, of course, that the biological evidence against this possibility was weighty, but he had to confess "in all modesty" that he simply could not proceed without the inheritance of acquired characters: "If things are different, then we are unable to advance one step further on our way, either in psychoanalysis or in mass psychology." [12] It would mean, in other words, that "facts" elicited in analysis were not facts at all. So, modern biology had to yield.

Moses and Monotheism and *Totem and Taboo* are among the most frequently cited examples of Freud's willingness to proceed with a thesis in the absence of corroborating evidence and in the face of contradictory evidence. But that might be only because he was telling histories in those works, and readers expect the testimony of witnesses to history. Elaborate analogies, fantasies about ontogeny recapitulating phylogeny, postulation of racial memories, images of microcosm and macrocosm, and a persistent drawing of far-fetched parallels between individual and social development as well as individual and social illness appear throughout his writings as standard parts of the argument. [13] His reiterated claim that stores of clinical data supported his very broad characterizations of human beings in general was seldom supported by systematic marshaling of those data. The reliability of the data themselves, although a matter of concern to him, was a problem never successfully handled by Freud. [14] He claimed a special status for "analytical reasoning," asserted that the truth in psychoanalytic theory can be evident only to those who have devoted their life to the theory and practice of psychoanalysis, and condescended on occasion to "help readers who are unwilling or unprepared to plunge into complicated psychological matters." [15] The "unwilling" here reminds us of those whom Calvin regarded as "unteachable" because of the unacknowledged sin within them, the implication being that if you do not understand and believe what I say, it is not because what I say is wrong or unconvincing, but because you are constitutionally incapable of believing it. When Freud attacked religions for appealing to a "court above reason" and represented psychoanalysis as only "a method of research, an impartial instrument,"[16] he was forgetting his dependence on myth and his often stubborn insistence on the correctness of an arch of conjecture whose keystone was an assumption required by its design.

Freud could be convincing in such maneuvers in part because of the peculiar attractiveness of arguments from mythology. If we seem to find in very old stories of distant and dramatic happenings a parallel, however obscure, to something here and now, the identity of the two cases and the universality of the phenomenon can be strongly suggested. Thus Toynbee took Mephistopheles' threat to destroy man as a challenge to which God responded with the whole drama of human existence. Toynbee then went on to say that all civilizations have arisen as responses to challenges, so elevating a mythical theme to the level of an eternal truth and a universal law of history.[17] When Freud created the story that all present anxiety is a repetition of birth trauma anxiety he used this convincing quality of myth. As Wittgenstein put it, this kind of explanation that something is the outcome of long-ago events is compelling—one is tempted to say, "Yes, of course, it must be like that."[18]

Careful fabrication of elaborate and fundamental instincts together with erudite mythological furnishing of the unconscious distinguish Freud as a sophisticated and highly imaginative human nature theorist. Yet, he was also capable on many occasions of the ordinary practice of simply putting into human nature whatever attributes a particular argument or prejudice called for. Thus, while he saw neurosis as a reaction to repression of basic drives, which he described in detail, his generally low estimate of people often was expressed simply in commonplace terms of human nature bashing. Humans were, in his judgment, a basically unruly bunch. They "exhibit an inborn tendency to carelessness, irregularity and unreliability in their work, and a laborious training is needed before they learn to follow the example of their celestial models."[19] The "masses" of people are "lazy and unintelligent" and support one another in "giving free rein to their indiscipline."[20] A "vast majority" of humans "need a high command to make decisions for them," to which they will "usually bow without demur."[21] Remarks such as these, together with his well-known reflections on the weakness of women, are entirely gratuitous, and they reveal that Freud's picture of human nature was not just a reproduction of psychoanalytic findings.

The extremes to which Freud was led by his gift of imagination and his inattention to rules of evidence are often set aside as idiosyncrasies that are irrelevant to his basic message. New versions or revisions of Freudian ideas to be found in object relations theory, ego psychology, interpersonal theory, and the like have little to do, apparently, with phylogenetic memory traces or the primordial crime. But so far as the question of human dignity is concerned, Freud had a point to make. The point was not new with him, and it did not die with him. The point was that people do not know what they are doing and are constitutionally incapable of consciously directing their life. That is a deep-seated myth in Western culture. Freud's contribution to the myth is significant.

[2]

Freud did not allow humans much dignity. This is evident in his outraged rejection of what he believed to be our high opinion of ourselves. A central feature of his work on religion is the message that people must give up the illusion of their importance and admit to themselves "the full extent of their helplessness and insignificance in the machinery of the universe."[22] He was dismayed by what he saw as people's blind refusal to acknowledge in themselves an instinct for aggression, and he explained their obstinacy by their fear of appearing sacrilegious. Belief in the goodness of human nature, Freud thought, is a religious presumption, "one of those evil illusions by which mankind expect their lives to be beautified and made easier while in reality they only cause damage." Pretending to love our enemies when actually we would like to see them hanged is self-deception. Our nature, he argued, makes it impossible for us to live up to anything like the Christian ethic.[23]

Freud wrote as if he were revealing for the first time the strong sexual and aggressive acts that figure so largely in human conduct and as if he would shock and offend everyone by the revelation. He repeatedly explained opposition to his views in these terms,[24] as though he were unaware that his disparaging remarks about human beings had been clearly anticipated by such predecessors as Montaigne, Rochefoucauld, Mandeville, Burton, and Swift. The common acceptance of vilifications of human nature—what Hilary Callan identified as the "public taste for castigation by experts"[25]— would seem to account rather for part of the widespread fascination with Freud.

How Freud could believe that religion, and especially Christianity, preached the goodness of humans is not clear. He might have confused the splendid image of pre-Fall Adam with the later totally depraved creature who is thought to be reproduced in each man and woman. But surely he was aware of a basic teaching of Christianity—and perhaps of any monotheism—that people are almost hopelessly and helplessly lost in evil, and that what they must do, far from basking in an illusion of their goodness, is confess their wickedness and their inability to escape the condition of sin on their own. What Freud said people must admit about themselves—their inner compulsion to violence and their inability to control it without the help of authority—is more than just reminiscent of John Calvin's message. Calvin's impatience with people who would not confess to what was really in them and accept the truth of their situation should have been understandable to Freud, whose patients seemed to stubbornly deny the hidden sources of their problems and who had to be convinced by authority that their troubles lay within themselves. He should have realized how similar his and Calvin's general estimates of human nature were and how alike were the problems of pastor and psychoanalyst in bringing ailing souls to see the light—a point not lost among some of the Christian clergy today.[26] Calvin's insistence on the damning hypocrisy of humans was, after all, an anticipation of Freud's point that we keep things hidden from ourselves; and both of them regarded an admission of this fact as a necessary first step in an escape from alienation. Calvin appreciated as much as Freud how people "dupe" themselves, hiding their vanity and falsehood in "crannies" of the human heart.[27] And both said denial of such frailties is in itself an indication of their terrible reality: to deny you are a hypocrite is simply hypocrisy; any claim to benevolence is a sign of selfishness; you lie when you say you are not a liar. To question the validity of this description of your humanness confirms its accuracy. Opposition to a doctrine about human nature is thus turned into evidence in support of it.

The compelling quality of both Calvin's and Freud's pictures of human nature derives in large part from their postulation of conduct-controlling forces *within* people. Finding in the human constitution the causes and explanations of what people think and do implies an inner force that must be expressed regardless of outer influences. Amelioration of the effects of such a force then appears doubtful or at least limited. The Augustinean and Calvinist idea of indwelling sin, of sin as a constituent part of every human, suggests an inevitable expression of its potential, as the presence of liver supposes bile ("The devil is never idle"). In some sophisticated theologies this notion is expressed by saying that sin presupposes itself.[28] In Christian doctrine the inherent, inescapable quality of evil and sin has been affirmed in the doctrine of original sin, and a more or less explicit imagery of inheritance from a first ancestor has been used to carry an impression of biological necessity.

Freud's story, though different in its symbols, adheres strongly to this theme of human nature as a collection of forces residing in people, forces that must, in one way or another, find expression. Those mythical entities, the instincts, are placed by Freud so deep within the human make-up that people deny their existence even in the obvious cases of aggression and eros. Variants like the death instinct, the compulsion to repeat or to restore an earlier or original state of things are even more profound, eluding even prolonged analytic probing.[29] Unlike the inward qualities of the fallen Adam and his progeny, the Freudian drives or instincts have been with the human race from its beginning, yet Freud's myth did contain an element similar to the Fall and its consequences. As recounted in *Totem and Taboo*, a sort of secular Genesis, an early crime was committed, and feelings of guilt for having killed the father descended as memories from the sons to all their successors and continue to burden us, as sin burdens all of Adam's descendants.[30]

The real significance of placing psychic qualities within the biological nature of people is that their force is thus rendered impervious to alteration and nearly beyond conscious control. The notion that our sins could be the result of our circumstances, and especially of our social circumstances, is anathema in Christian theology. That would rob sin of its "originality." In the judgment of Protestant theologians like Reinhold Niebuhr such a belief amounts to social determinism;[31] and Calvin would not allow misfortune, much less ignorance, to explain sin. Freud followed in this tradition when he was very reluctant to grant the possibility that any kind of individual effort or social reform could tame instinctual forces in people.

But the question of fatalism in Freud's thinking—the question of whether or to what extent men and women can act to alter their tragic situation—is a matter of some dispute in Freudian scholarship. It is an important problem, for humankind's thralldom to an imperious nature is at stake.

The argument focuses, in one respect, on Freud's conception of the unconscious, the centerpiece of his system. It is certainly possible to say that Freud's teaching and practice aimed at enabling people to become aware of the contents of their unconscious and so to make it possible to deal with them. The therapy situation implies this: let the analyst find out what in your unconscious is disturbing you, bring you to recognize and acknowledge it, and thus make it possible for you to deal rationally with it and so free yourself from its baleful influences. The extent to which this is possible—the rate of "cures" among cases—is problematic within and outside the profession, and the relevance of the matter to the validity of psychoanalytic theory is also questioned. Larger questions concerning the practical possibility of analysis for significant numbers of people or the effectiveness of self-analysis have been raised as well. Such considerations, however, are tangential to deeper problems presented by the unconscious as it was conceived by Freud.

In his more serious (or gloomier, or later in life) moments, the unconscious as a force in human life became all-encompassing for

Freud. Now it was not just a matter of some hysterical female suffering from hidden memories of an early sexual experience, or a young
man not realizing he wanted to kill father and possess mother. Nor
was it only a universal racial memory producing an engulfing feeling of guilt. Beyond all this Freud saw basic tragedy in the entire
human life drama. People by their very nature need and want au-
thoritative discipline, and people by their very nature hate and resist
authority. They are unruly, and they need rules. Social controls are
required to keep the expression of powerful human erotic and aggressive drives within necessary bounds, and society makes people
sick by controlling them. People are thus required by their nature to
live in circumstances that deny their nature—here is the basic and
tragic contradiction in the human condition.[32]

The problem, as Freud saw it, is complicated and worsened when
people deny its existence, deny it by hiding from themselves what
lies deep in their inner being and really motivates them. They reject
their sexuality and their destructiveness by thinking of themselves
as moved only by unselfish benevolence or other lofty motives; they
profess an ethic that they do not want to obey and cannot obey. They
refuse to recognize the desperateness of their situation even as they
drive themselves to erotic and aggressive indulgences that they will
not acknowledge as such but disguise as tenderness and altruism.

The unconscious for Freud is not, then, just a hiding place for
troublesome thoughts engendered by trauma or misfortune or mis-
deed. It contains, rather, the real substance of human living, the
polarities and contradictions of an existence that denies itself. For
Freud, what is real about human life is lodged in the unconscious,
and it was there that psychoanalytic inquiry sought reality.

It was difficult for Freud to entertain a high regard for a being
he had placed in such a disastrous situation. What could men and
women do? Sublimation of instinctual drives was a possibility. Actual
tenderness of feeling and response could derive from a reduction
of the sexual impulse.[33] Aggression was for Freud a need more difficult, though not impossible, to divert.[34] Generally speaking, however, sublimation was not offered by Freud as an effective escape
from the instincts. It did not satisfy the individual as direct indul-

gence did. Freud had set up a clear conflict between potent instinctual forces and commanding social repression; harmonious adjust-
ment was not to be achieved by halfway measures.[35]

If therapy for the particular individual problem and sublimation as a very limited attenuation of the general instinctual pressure
could not cope with the massive human dilemma, were there, then,
social or cultural solutions? Freud's obvious equivocation about
this possibility is an understandable consequence of his having
cast society or civilization as both the villain in his myth and the
only really effective disciplinarian of a tempestuous human nature.
Society made people sick, and Freud showed considerable sympathy for the patients. Still, humans presumably wanted as well as
needed social coercion. The dilemma pressed at every level.

Freud left an opening of sorts, however, one that has been
exploited by some neo-Freudians. The individual is profoundly
shaped, he argued, by childhood experiences. Early relations with
both parents produce love-hate feelings that are difficult to resolve
and sometimes result in more or less severe neuroses. A person is
to this extent, then, not given at birth; human nature is in some respects shaped by social experience instead of being only an unfolding of innate potential. Although Freud thought the essential features of this experience were universal, there was still the possibility
of mitigating its adverse effects by means other than merely allay-
ing the symptoms. Deliberately changing the social circumstances
of child-rearing, and of human relations generally, can be seen,
from this point of view, as a way of consciously taking an active part
in shaping human life, and it is clear enough that Freud has shown
object relations theorists such as Nancy Chodorow a way in such an
undertaking.[36]

As is so often the case with Freud, it is difficult to reconcile this
side of his argument with another. The special perturbations that
he saw arising from childhood trauma appear relatively minor when
compared with the awful contradictions of the life and death instincts and the broader depiction of human existence as a process
bent inexorably on negating itself. Freeing the person from, say,
an Oedipus complex does not constitute freedom from an organic

nature doomed to return to an inorganic state. It is not, of course, necessary to take Freud at his gloomiest, and there is little use in demanding consistency. Yet, Philip Rieff had a point when he chided "liberal" ameliorists with simply ignoring the essential Freud, the profound and daring and revolutionary Freud, when they proposed superficial palliatives for utter tragedy.[37] There is, in any event, an integral part of the Freudian doctrine that carries on and elaborates the oppressive traditional myth of a basic organic flaw in humankind.

Erich Fromm and others have tried to defend Freud against charges of historical determinism or fatalism by pointing to signs of hope in such writings as *Future of an Illusion* and *Why War?* Earlier, Freud had held out the possibility that ego could one day prevail over id and bring an element of rational planning and conduct into human life.[38] And at the general level of social life Freud could be cautiously optimistic on occasion. Thus in his analysis of religion and rejection of its empty promises Freud evidently felt an obligation to offer something in its place. Science, or a complete devotion to reason, provided a hope that "a re-ordering of human relations should be possible, which would remove the sources of dissatisfaction with civilization by renouncing coercion and the suppression of the instincts, so that, undisturbed by internal discord, men might devote themselves to the acquisition of wealth and its enjoyment."[39] Science, he went on, can give us knowledge about the world "by means of which we can increase our power and in accordance with which we can arrange our life."[40] People can be educated out of their futile dependence on religion, leave the infantile orientation to existence, and use their intellectual powers to achieve a reorganization of their social life. The overwhelming tyranny of instinctual drives seems suddenly, and unaccountably, blunted when Freud tells us: "We may insist as often as we like that man's intellect is powerless in comparison with his instinctual life, and we may be right in this. Nevertheless, there is something peculiar about the weakness. The voice of the intellect is a soft one, but it does not rest till it has found a hearing. Finally, after a countless succession of rebuffs, it succeeds. This is one of the few points on which one may be optimistic about the future of mankind. . . . in the long run nothing can withstand reason and experience."[41]

One must anticipate that Freud would hedge these observations with provisos, negating qualifications, and outright contradictions. His basic position called for it. In a postscript to his *Autobiographical Study,* Freud told us that when he returned from detours in natural science, medicine, and psychotherapy to his original interest in cultural matters, he could see that the events of human history "are no more than a reflection of dynamic conflicts between the ego, the id and the superego, which psycho-analysis studies in the individual."[42] If cultural life is but an enlarged version of the terrible individual life struggle depicted by Freud, a rosy historical scenario is not to be expected. So, an experiment in scientific instead of religious education could fail, Freud granted, and he was ready to return to his *"purely descriptive* judgment" that humans are weak in intelligence and ruled by instinct.[43] Having deprived the public of rationality, Freud could not seriously consider a possibility of community action for a rationally ordered social life free of coercion: "It seems rather that every civilization must be built up on coercion and renunciation of instinct; it does not even seem certain that if coercion were to cease the majority of human beings would be prepared to undertake to perform the work necessary for acquiring new wealth."[44] Hope for a solution to such a problem as war must, then, be tempered by realization that "the inclination to aggression is an original, self-subsisting instinctual disposition in man," and that "there is no likelihood of our being able to suppress humanity's aggressive tendencies." War, indeed, seems to be "a natural thing enough, biologically sound and practically unavoidable."[45]

Freud eventually came to a kind of statistical compromise about the possibility of a better human future. He spoke of the "extent" to which the burden of instinctual sacrifice might be lightened and the "percentage of mankind" who might come to be less asocial and less hostile to civilization. Turning what is now the majority of people who are unfit for civilization into a minority is, Freud concluded, "perhaps all that *can* be accomplished."[46]

It was in the context of this discussion of a future in which human beings might achieve a larger measure of conscious, rational control of their lives that Freud returned to a characteristic elitism and to a related and always present but vague evolutionism.

As noted earlier, an elitist stance is necessarily implied in a thinker who declares that people are intellectually impotent and morally depraved: one must somehow be an exception—be honest and able— if the statement is to be credited. Freud saw himself as qualified in part by having gone through a special enabling process, psychoanalysis. It would be a mistake, however, to say that he saw analysis as the only or even the chief way in which people could become better fitted for civilized social life. Generally speaking, he believed intelligence to be the basic control of instinctual nature,[47] and the small group of analyzed people had no monopoly on intelligence. Self-control through reason was not limited to the formal therapeutic session. Intelligent people, however, and those whose ability for self-control qualified them to educate others, constituted, Freud was sure, a rather small minority. Most people "have no love for instinctual renunciation" and cannot be convinced by argument that renunciation must come. No matter what is done, "a certain percentage of mankind (owing to a pathological disposition or an excess of instinctual strength)" will remain hostile to civilization. Leaders who possess "superior insight into the necessities of life and who have risen to the height of mastering their own instinctual wishes" can set an example for the masses and serve as their educators, but even then cultural change can be effected in people only with an "enormous amount of coercion." The great majority of people are "dangerous" and must be "held down most severely" until they are psychically prepared to substitute reason for a fear of God in control of their conduct.[48]

Freud had serious misgivings, then, about how much could be accomplished how quickly in the civilizing process by the example and teaching of a dedicated and rationally prepared elite. His uncertainty did not derive just from caution or his usual pessimism, however, for he tentatively presented in the context of this discussion a notion of how an elite arises out of the mass of irrational humankind and how the whole of the human race goes through a natural process in which rational control of instinctual forces emerges to produce a peaceful social life free of neurosis-producing coercion. In his somewhat vague and sometimes wistful references to such a process Freud came to a general expression of an evolutionist perspective that had colored much of his earlier work.[49]

He had included nineteenth- and early twentieth-century cultural evolutionists in his omnivorous reading. The grand reconstructions of a James George Frazer clearly appealed to Freud's taste for myth—for explanation of a present condition in terms of origins hidden in a remote past and pregnant with all the future.[50] The dramatic story created by Freud in *Totem and Taboo* is almost a caricature of the genre.

In *Civilization and Its Discontents* Freud broached a question of whether human "cultural development" would in time result in control of the instinctual aggressiveness that plagued communal life.[51] In *Why War?* the point was made with regard to the possibility of an emerging pacifism as a next stage in human evolution. He continued his earlier argument about the prospect of a handful of enlightened men overcoming their aggressive drives and serving as role models and instructors in an eventual conversion of others to pacifism.[52] Now he went on, however, to speculate on the problem of how enlightenment had come to the elite, and his answer was that a biological process had been at work to bring it about. It was not a question of who had taught the teachers; a few people had experienced "a progressive rejection of instinctual ends and a scaling down of instinctive reactions." This was an organic process as he saw it; there were organic grounds for the changes in the ethical and aesthetic ideals of the enlightened. Freud was talking at the outset about himself and Albert Einstein (the discussion of war takes place in a letter to Einstein) as representatives of this elite, and about their role in leading others to the light. Perhaps the question of why this organic process had affected so few had to be faced. In any event. he moved on to see the process of cultural evolution as a universal movement, the "cultural development of mankind." But not all of mankind at the same time. One sign of cultural evolution, Freud believed, is an impairment of the sexual function. So, "uncivilized races and backward classes of all nations" reveal the incompleteness of the cultural process by "multiplying more rapidly than the cultured elements."[53]

The unevenness of the progressive cultural process was, of course, a standard tenet of European evolutionism, and the idea fitted well with Freud's belief that "primitive" peoples (that is, non-European, nonliterate colonials) represented an early stage in psychic development, a stage also represented by the civilized child and, in some respects, by civilized women. What the mechanism of this evolutionary process might be seems not to have concerned Freud. There was no suggestion of natural selection of variations carrying reproductive advantage. There was no recourse here to the idea of inheritance and accumulation of acquired cultural characters to account for a kind of Lamarckian progress. Freud did not speculate about any cause for or meaning in the process. It was left as a blind movement in which decisions and choices by people played no part.[54] The engines of cultural change had traditionally been left obscure by evolutionists; Freud's postulation of vague organic sources did nothing to improve the situation.

So far as the ability of humans to consciously and rationally control their social conduct is concerned, then, Freud finally came to see this as a direct consequence of organic change, not as a result of education or therapy, not as a product of human action, not as an outcome of social and cultural change. The process of cultural evolution whereby the human species comes to control its life and enjoy a relatively peaceful existence was, for Freud, a parallel to the normal development of the individual human psyche: "we cannot fail to be struck by the similarity between the processes of civilization and the libidinal development of the individual."[55]

Having made his detour through natural science to grapple with cultural concerns, Freud brought with him the biological luggage that had always accompanied him. He stayed with his objective of finding an organic basis for all psychic phenomena. He apparently saw no slight to Albert Einstein's dignity or to his own when he cooly observed that they opposed war only because they could not help doing so; they were pacifists because their "organic nature" willed

them to be pacifists,[56] while less developed people, by clear implication, welcomed war and were militarists for organic reasons also.
Ethical choices are reduced to biological differences.

Despite Freud's occasional suggestions that human beings can
come to take charge of their lives as individuals and as members of a
society, the heavy burdens of the unconscious with which he saddled
them made the task too difficult. Therapy is not a practical vehicle
to the general end. Social reform and education cannot cope with
forces that lie so deep within the organism. Science cannot overcome the tragedy of human nature. When Calvin deprived humans
of free will—of any ability to form choices and act on them—he
rendered them helpless before their incomprehensible God. When
Freud hid or disguised all human willing and choosing and aims of
action in the unconscious he effectively made people just as helpless
and could try to rescue them only with a vague and still incomprehensible deus ex machina, evolution. His resort to this device was
not just a part of the pessimism of old age, and not a momentary
aberration from a vision of id succumbing to ego. Freud had judged
humans to be incapable of dealing with the basic realities of their
situation, and it was only consistent of him to recognize, finally, that
he owed his own limited victory to an organic process that he could
not help experiencing.

This affront to human dignity is ultimate. Calvin submitted
people to God, who "has a hidden bridle by which he restrains furious beasts so that they cannot break out wherever their mad appetite impels them." Montaigne warned us that "it is safer to leave the
reins of conduct in the hands of Nature than to keep them in our
own." Edward O. Wilson more recently assured us that the "genes
hold culture on a leash."[57] Freud made humans thrall to nature by
tying their escape from organic commands to a biological process
of evolution in which they are objects, not actors.

CHAPTER FIVE

Social Science and Human Agency

T HE ATTEMPT of modern students of society to apply methods of natural science in their work has done much to sustain and elaborate the Western belief in human impotence —in this case a belief that people are incapable of deliberately and rationally shaping their social and cultural life.

By the close of the seventeenth century the natural science enterprise had gone far in reducing humankind to insignificance in a vast and meaningless mechanical universe. This only confirmed in some ways the Reformation image of the human as a "five-foot worm," but there was a new element in the picture. Where Calvin's poor specimen was reduced to near nullity by virtue of being so far inferior to God, now the human being was stripped of dignity by being cast as merely one more natural object among an infinity of other objects and of no more concern to God than any other thing. Science gave *Homo* a place in the order of things, but the order was no longer regarded as the product of an intelligence in whose image Adam had been created. Belief in an anthropomorphic God who created and moved all things according to a plan was replaced with the idea of a universe as a system in itself, with its own laws, self-produced and functioning according to principles inherently its own. Scientific method sought only to identify objective factors, forces, or processes that would reveal and explain systematic relationships among natural events. People now found themselves in an order of contingency with no intention behind it, no purpose, no meaning.[1]

If this new way of representing the natural world was a blow to ideas of human importance, the program to extend such concepts and procedures to the study of human activity itself had even more serious consequences for lingering Renaissance visions of human dignity. For now the objective was to grasp human social and cultural life also as a system in which something other than human agency—causes other than intentional human acts—are responsible for historical results. The alternative of taking people more as objects shaped by society than as subjects who make their society came to prevail. Now people were left out of social processes not so much because it is difficult to accommodate unruly Hobbesian creatures in a smoothly functioning social order, but because these unpredictable humans are no longer needed as social actors and can be replaced by objective, integrating, equilibrating forces.

There is a tension in modern social science between attempts to implement this scientific outlook and efforts to bring people back in to conceptions of social action—a tension between positivism and humanism, between an emphasis on structure or human agency. Although it is no longer customary to accompany these different approaches with different explicit images of human nature, the different images are still clearly implied.

[1]

Jeremy Bentham's *Introduction to the Principles of Morals and Legislation* (1789) signaled the positivistic social theory to come. By investing humans with behavior-producing forces that were supposed to be quantitatively calculable, and by limiting the forces to a simple positive desire for pleasure and a negative avoidance of pain, Bentham seemed to have reduced people to the status of natural objects whose "motions" could be described and explained in Newtonian fashion. Considerations of utility were taken not only to account for people's actions but also as defensible moral principles.[2]

The positive philosophy of Auguste Comte (1798–1857) and synthetic philosophy of Herbert Spencer (1820–1903), although not

founded on simplistic ideas of human motivation, nonetheless formalized and provided much of the outline of the great nineteenth-
century European effort to bring science to bear on an explica-
tion of social order and social change. A reiterated objective of this
enterprise was to escape the barren empiricism of traditional his-
toriography and its concentration on the doings of great men, and
to penetrate instead to the basic "statics" and "dynamics" of society,
as Comte put it in his "social physics" (the earlier name he gave to
sociology). Spencer's imagery was more biological. In fact, when he
described society as an organism he cautioned us not to suppose
this was mere metaphor; the structure, functions, and development
of society, he insisted, were not different from the anatomy, physi-
ology, and evolution of other organisms. And what the scientific
sociologist must scrupulously avoid, Spencer continued, is an attribution of causal agency to either the workings of providence or the
motives of humans.[3]

The absence of human actors is most striking in nineteenth-
century accounts of social and cultural evolution. This process was
depicted by positivists as a direct product of progressive principles
identified, rather loosely, in the human or in the social organism,
and, again in general terms, ontogeny was taken to recapitulate phylogeny. Attention to specific persons or peoples or to times when
and places where was regarded as not only unnecessary but actually
a distraction from the task of discerning general principles or laws
at work. The question of why social and cultural change occurred
when and where it did was seldom raised. Instead, the aim was
to identify origins and stages and to "people" these with examples
chosen from the historical and ethnographic record and arranged
in a series according to an a priori concept of gradual change from
the undifferentiated to the differentiated in form and function. The
product was very much like earlier philosophies of history, but now
with the trappings of scientific discourse added.[4]

The positivist heritage has left traces and strains in modern social
science. There are three major ways in which effective human actors
have been removed from the social scene: (1) by contending that objective elements in social structure rather than subjective intentions

and actions play the greater part in producing social consequences; (2) by holding that people as such cannot make society because people are only reflections of their social existence; and (3) by arguing that deliberate human actions are beside the point because the social consequences of human actions are largely unintended. The implication of all three themes is that men and women are powerless inasmuch as they have no conscious, deliberate, reasoned control over the course of their social life and cultural work. The following testimony from social scientists themselves bears on these points.

It is ironic that one of the most notable efforts in social science to restore people as actors in history had the apparent effect of promoting social structures or systems as the effective historical agents. In 1937 the American sociologist Talcott Parsons discerned and sought to encourage a movement in recent social thought toward recognition of the part played by human will, decision, and effort in social action. He reminded us that the norms and ideals held by men and women are something other than a bland cultural *condition* of their lives. As ideals they represent something that people *strive* to realize, possibilities that stir action and *effort* on their part, the "creative or voluntaristic" side of social life that positivists had forgotten in their preoccupation with "passive, adaptive, receptive" attitudes.[5] It is difficult to assess the extent to which Parsons might have been misinterpreted or later changed his position, thus giving "structural functionalism" a different set of objectives in sociological study, but it is the case that he has been widely regarded as responsible for a proliferation of efforts to conceptualize societies as systems not involving human actions of any kind, much less voluntary actions.

Thus George Homans (Parson's colleague at Harvard University at the time) took the occasion of his presidential address to the American Sociological Association to make a plea for "bringing men back in" to analysis of social phenomena instead of trying to derive explanations of human activity from abstractions such as roles, social equilibria, systems, and institutions. However necessary or useful it might be to conceive of groups of social facts as institutions and then to detect relationships of institutions in concrete historical situations, those conceptions cannot, Homans pointed out, serve to account for human actions. Societies, he reminded Parsons and his students, do not have needs, only people do. Explanatory theories must therefore be about the behavior of humans, ultimately, not about social structures. The alternative is an image of society in which there are no actors and no action. The implication of Homans's remarks (which he went on to make quite explicit before his audience of sociologists) is that we must turn to psychology instead of sociology for explanations of human social conduct simply because sociologists have chosen to ignore real live people in the study of society.[6]

While Homans's plea for bringing people back in to social science arose from methodological concerns about how social facts are to be explained, others have been more interested in the moral implications of recognizing humans as free to lead social lives of their own devising and choosing.[7] So Ralf Dahrendorf observed that sociologists, though fairly successful in efforts to demonstrate that society is indeed a fact, have lost sight of Kant's autonomous and free person and have let the unique individual with his claim to respect and dignity elude them. In place of the undetermined person who possesses "some irreducible measure of freedom to act as he chooses," sociologists, according to Dahrendorf, have erected a *Homo sociologicus* who is no more than a set of useful analytical concepts. Then they have, almost absentmindedly it would seem, confused the model with the real thing, and the result is a misleading impression of having described human nature when only *Homo sociologicus* has been defined. Thus a "moral image of the human person" is lost, and sociology becomes "a thoroughly inhuman, amoral science."[8]

Homans and Dahrendorf did not press the question of how, even in the midst of a sociological endeavor to build respect for human effort and will in social action, human moral activity came to be ignored. One possible reason is that sociologists have been dedicated, at least since Émile Durkheim's day, to a demonstration of how people acquire what could be called a second nature of sociableness by internalizing a set of norms that regulate their social conduct. This solution to the Hobbesian problem without resort to Lord Shaftesbury's postulation of a social propensity served a purpose, but sociologists have sometimes given the process of socialization such effectiveness that individuals are reduced to a status of passive objects. Recognition of the importance of social experience in the shaping of human beings appears to have led on to a kind of determinism that is just what Parsons was anxious to avoid in his conception of a voluntaristic system of action. In our efforts to escape simplistic (and often mischievous) biological or biopsychological explications of the social or cultural, we have given Society and Culture a reality and power that excludes persons and raises the specter of a dread "subjectivism" in the human sciences whenever humans are introduced as effective and deliberate actors. Then components of analytical systems take the place of people in history and a presumably scientific procedure of seeking the "real" productive forces behind the epiphenomena of human acts is followed.

We appear to be fascinated by this notion of something going on "behind people's backs," something known only to experts.[9] Experts foster the idea, of course, but the laity seems to welcome it with or without scientific sanction. We speak of the inevitability of war, the irreversible growth of bureaucracy ("you can't beat City Hall"), the inescapable business cycle, and the irresistible march of science. We know the poor will always be with us, and we speak of doings that have no doers—the dropping of the bomb, the fouling of the environment, the destruction of inner cities.

In an effort to pursue a rigorous science of society by interposing ideal constructs between ourselves and our acting human subjects we have, then, not only made it difficult to arrive at genuine explanations of social facts but we have also fostered a myth about humans that precludes moral inquiry and value judgments.

A closely related form of social determinism is associated with the quite legitimate effort to demonstrate and appreciate the fact that men and women cannot become what we observe them to be unless they interact with others in a society and have the support of a culture. We tend to forget, again, how an awareness of this sociocultural dimension of human life was developed in countering beliefs that people and, especially, differences among people, are basically products of organic constitution and physical environment. It is perhaps a consequence of the strong and misleading appeal of the biological argument that social science has carried an emphasis on social and cultural influences to the point of another determinism. The result, according to some social scientists, is a reduction of people to robots who automatically accept and act in accordance with any prevailing code of conduct or fashion.

Seeking to rescue a measure of autonomy and selfhood for individuals, the sociologist Dennis Wrong has accused his colleagues of trying to bypass the Hobbesian problem by representing people as "oversocialized" creatures who cannot pose any threat to social order inasmuch as they are only products of that social order, bent upon seeking the approval of others. To Wrong, this kind of social determinism denies the reality of an inherent humanness that resents and resists and suffers from outside attempts to control or to alter it. The Hobbesian human being, from this Freudian point of view, does not quietly bow to Leviathan; there is a continuing struggle between them, and doubt remains about the possibility of any system of social control in which a person can be entirely at peace with either him- or herself or with others.[10]

In a similar vein, Harold Garfinkel has pointed to a tendency among social science theorists to render people "judgmental dopes": cultural dopes who simply reproduce a society by following lines of action prescribed by a common culture, and psychological dopes who maintain the stable features of a society by pursuing courses of action dictated by "psychiatric biography, conditioning history, and the variables of mental functioning." A member of society is thus said to be left with no choice, no subjectivity, no judgment—"culture bound and need compelled."[11]

Social theories that either replace active people with objective structures or make men and women into social automata contribute, then, to the long record of denial of human dignity. The old and persisting belief, however, that the consequences of people's social activity are not what people intend them to be has probably worked a more fundamental breach of confidence in human power to act purposefully and intelligently in the conduct of human affairs.

The paradox of human actions having results (either good or

bad) quite different from what the actors intended has, as we have seen, long attracted the attention of Western scholars. Every thinker of note since Vico, apparently, has commented on the phenomenon and has taken a position regarding it. The subject is raised when concrete problems of social planning and control are taken up, when larger questions concerning the direction and meaning of history are pursued, and, generally, when the possibilities and means of a science of society are considered.

When intentional human social acts have consequences quite different from those sought by the actors, observers are often so struck by this perversity or paradox that they are inclined to attribute the consequences to such abstractions as ideas or social forces and structures that produce their effect through the actions of individuals who do not comprehend what is going on. These abstractions, presented in metaphors like Adam Smith's invisible hand and Hegel's cunning of reason, served at first as secular substitutes for an active God or providence, and they often still seem to be regarded as mysteries of independent standing that should not be questioned and before which we must humbly submit. This habit of thought is most striking among some economists. In extreme cases people are admonished to renounce the fallacious belief that "the human mind is . . . superior to natural social processes" or that it is capable of shaping institutional forms.[12] We must, therefore, (as Montaigne put it) acknowledge our incapacity and submit to nature with confidence that we are in good hands. F. H. Knight, in a classic statement of this doctrine, warned that people cannot make society by their deliberate acts and that chance must be seen as more than human ignorance about causality—it is "an unanalyzable fact of nature."[13] Although Hayek thought it a mistake to explain persistent social structures as products of either mysterious external powers or conscious human design, the frailty of human reason was still the central feature of his case against deliberate social planning or action. The complexity of combined individual acts in the market, he argued, simply cannot be grasped by any human mind; and yet he thought that we can know that these independent acts, if unimpeded by collective restraint, produce coherent structures that serve desirable human purposes they were not intended to serve.[14] We seem to be left, then, with a social theory that must never be taken as a program of action—with a knowledge about our social life that tells us not to tamper with its basic nature.

Sociologists have long regarded a recognition of unintended or unanticipated outcomes of intentional social action as a special insight. Robert Merton wrote an influential essay on the subject early in his career and then went on to develop the idea in his identification of manifest and latent functions of actions for social systems.[15] Merton's belief that unintended consequences constitute the heart of sociology's subject matter is widely shared. Louis Schneider saw Mandeville's interest in paradoxes and the Scottish moral philosophers' general sensitivity to unanticipated results as important foundations of both functionalism and evolutionism in modern sociology. Schneider voiced a common opinion when he said, "It is hardly credible that a social science worth its salt will ever assign an insignificant place to phenomena of this kind."[16] Piotr Sztompka calls unintended consequences the "real mechanisms" of the social system as opposed to the "ideal."[17] Smelser and Warner appear to speak for the profession when they describe the concept of unanticipated consequences of social action as one of the "great intellectual contributions of the sociological point of view."[18] Speaking more generally, Charles Taylor observes that a category like "the cunning of reason," far from being a peculiarly Hegelian mystical idea, is "indispensable for any theory of history which wants to give a role to unconscious motivation." The implication of all this for human dignity is revealed by Taylor when he says, "For Hegel . . . man is never clear what he is doing at the time; for the agency is not simply man. We are all caught up as agents in a drama we do not really understand."[19]

Now it is clear enough that people often act to bring about things they did not intend to bring about. Robert Burns spoke the obvious when he said, "The best laid schemes o' mice an' men Gang aft a-gley." We recognize this as a common occurrence in both private and public life, are aware that our acts have in the past led to results that we did not expect, and are always more or less engaged in trying to draw on our experience so as to shape action to achieve what we mean it to achieve. It is also evident that a contriving of better "laid schemes" often calls for a more careful and extensive marshaling and consideration of experience than most poeple in the going concern of life have time for, and it is appropriate that reliable knowledge of this kind be sought by people who do have the time to prepare for the task.

But it can be misleading and troublesome to elevate Burns's homely observation to the status of a historical force, endow it with causal agency, and suggest that it designates the subject matter of the social sciences. When the invisible-hand story is stripped of its striking paradoxes—its illusion of magical results—unintended consequences of social action turn out to be no more than unexplained consequences, something people do not understand. That raises a question of why they do not understand—why they do not correctly anticipate what will result from their action. How the question is answered has implications for our ideas about human worth and dignity.

One answer is that humans are simply incapable of understanding their social life because of their limited intellectual powers, or because social life is so complex, or because of some combination of the two. Since this judgment, if taken seriously, simply forecloses discussion, it has no place in any forum of social inquiry.

So, another response is suggested: people do not correctly foresee what happens because what happens is not a direct result of their individual intentional actions, but of a complex combination of those actions that was not, and cannot be, planned. This is where the market or the social structure or some other feature of the system is called upon to explain consequences not understandable as products of purposeful human acts. Acting persons are, indeed, involved, but they do not know what they are doing.

Now the question is: *Can* human beings, in the conduct of their social life know how to act in ways that will get the results they want? Does the problem of unintended consequences turn on this point of what people are capable of knowing?

Merton appears to have come to just this position: people do not correctly anticipate because they do not know enough about the relations of acts and consequences. "The most obvious limitation to a correct anticipation of consequences is provided by the existing state of knowledge"[20]—not, it should be noticed, by the operation of incomprehensible natural forces. Although Merton went on to say that our errors, our tendency to allow pressing interests to interfere with our thinking, and our failure to note how even our anticipations of consequences also combine to limit our ability to foresee— all of these are general conditions of an existing state of knowledge. His occasional surrender to complexities "quite beyond our reach" could hardly be a resting place for a scholar who is seriously engaged in an examination of human social life. It becomes clear (as Campbell has pointed out)[21] in Merton's later discussion of manifest and latent functions that unintended consequences are to be identified only by improved knowledge about relations of intentional acts and their results. There is no suggestion of probing mysteries in order to reveal the machinery of paradoxes or the irony of history. Manifest consequences of acts are easily known; latent consequences are, by definition, more difficult to connect with specific acts.

It is clear, furthermore, that Merton would have no truck with a notion that latent consequences of acts are somehow knowable only by a special category of people such as sociologists and other experts. People find out what people find out, and though some people find out more than other people, the knowable and the unknowable are not defined by the existence of different kinds of people.

Karl Popper's forthright reaction to the reality of unintended consequences clearly undercuts the myth of dark forces obscuring people's vision of what they are doing. The fact of unforeseen results in the past, he pointed out, simply calls for an effort to foresee results in the future. Popper knows we often act in ways that yield results we did not anticipate; he even grants that experience indicates we probably always shall to some extent. But he properly insists on a perspective from which results of action, whatever they are, must be understood as products of the concrete doings of people, not of abstract conditions of action.[22]

There is a sense, of course, in which the results of social inquiry and reflection—whether professional or lay—are always revelations of unintended or unanticipated consequences of our activities. To discover previously undetected relationships between social action events and subsequent conditions or events is to show, perforce, that the people then involved in the action were not fully aware of what the results of their acts would be. This is no more paradoxical or ironic than the common personal experience of not "meaning" to have actually brought about some regrettable thing by one's acts and then resolving, on reflection, to act differently in the future. What we learn from more or less systematic observation of experience is how to anticipate relationships between acts and consequences we had not before anticipated. But to leap from a recognition of this integral feature of social life to a conclusion that people *generally* do not know what they are doing is quite unwarranted. The tendency of social scientists to represent unintended consequences as a prevailing and ineradicable feature of social action can easily contribute to the persistent Western myth that men and women are powerless pawns in a drama they neither plot nor direct.

[2]

There have been serious efforts to escape the determinism that has accompanied the program to construct a natural science of human group life. Misgivings about positivist social inquiry were expressed in Georg Simmel's concept of the autonomous individual engaged in social interaction, in Émile Durkheim's studied attempt to recapture the idea of a moral order in which people played active roles, and in Max Weber's depiction of concrete historical contexts where people acted from conviction. There were these and many other signs of an unease about a human science that had lost sight of human beings.

When we look, however, among modern social theorists for the most striking endowment of people with a power to construct their social world according to a rational plan of action, Karl Marx must come first to mind. And it is in Marx, perhaps, that we can discern most clearly a tension between the quest for a rigorous science of social life and a recognition of the need for purposive human activity in both a theory of and a practical realization of historical social changes.

Marx tried to show how real men and women rather than an abstract reason or a market force make history and can remake society. He agreed with Vico's idea that human activity is the only source of the social and cultural world and that the human mind can therefore comprehend that world in all its complexity. Marx struck the most effective modern blow against mystifying notions of things other than humans producing the substance and circumstances of their existence. He called such beliefs alienating inasmuch as they separated people from the effects of their thought and work and substituted in their place abstractions that are the impotent dream products of philosophers. When idealists paraded their Hegelian abstractions as active forces in the world, Marx thundered, *"History* does *nothing,* 'it possesses *no* immense wealth,' it 'wages no battles.' It is *man,* real, living man who does all that, who possesses and fights; 'history' is not, as it were, a person apart, using man as a means to achieve *its own* aims; history is *nothing but* the activity of man pursuing his aims."[23]

Yet our legacy from Marx is mixed on the question of human historical effectiveness. Marx's call for human action was accompanied by an undertaking to replace ideology with a scientific demonstration of historical circumstances in which the action must take place. People "make their own history," but, Marx quickly added, "they do not make it just as they please; they do not make it under circumstances chosen by themselves, but under circumstances directly found, given and transmitted from the past."[24] On occasion Marx would describe the constraining features of capitalism as weighty circumstances indeed. Then the economic formation of society is portrayed as "a process of natural history" in which "natural laws of capitalist production" work "with iron necessity towards inevitable results." What was happening to English people in the 1860s would happen later to German people, apparently no matter what they did.[25] A "leading thread" in his studies, Marx tells us, was a conviction that "in the social production process which men carry on they enter into definite relations that are indispensable and independent of their will."[26]

These different messages in Marx can be understood in terms of an early and late Marx, or as referring to conditions before and after the establishment of a classless society, or simply as variations in a rich and dynamic body of thought. It seems fair to judge the variety, however, as in some measure an outcome of combining a call to deliberate action with an attempt to give scientific credibility to the practicality of the action. Later forms of Marxian thought reflect this equivocality. The demands of Althusser's structuralism left little room for anything like independent action by subjects, while Lukács and Gramsci were obviously seeking to revive the voluntarist strains in Marx's thinking.[27] The extent to which any of this involved a return to or abandonment of a "true" Marxist position is beside the point of interest here. The dispute is one more indication of the confusion surrounding efforts to construct a human science that comprehends deliberate human activity, a dilemma resulting in part from the combination of an abiding mythology of human helplessness and a practical concern to find guidance for a planned reconstruction of human societies. The important point for a discussion of human nature mythology is that Marx seems not to have generally burdened human beings with an incapacity for understanding and acting effectively upon the circumstances of their lives. "False consciousness" was a result of a particular historical experience, not a universal or inherent human condition. People were alienated in the sense that they did not recognize their power, not in the sense that they were powerless.[28]

The problem of theory and practice is evident again in recent efforts by French sociologists to bring people back in to purposive social action, efforts that illustrate both a renewed belief in human agency and gnawing doubts about people's ability to understand what they are doing. Alain Touraine, encouraged by the promise of student and worker movements of the 1960s, was among the first to herald and encourage the "return of the actor" to the contemporary social scene.[29] Convinced that the workers' battle against the contradictions of capitalism can no longer be the locus of social change in postindustrial society, Touraine identifies a new kind of social movement, or melange of social movements, aimed at an emancipation of people from technocratic controls that go far beyond mere economic exploitation and seek rather to dominate ethical, artistic, sexual, and all other aspects of life experience. Touraine accepts Marx's idea that people make their own society, but he insists that they do so by their free activity and not along paths set by the kind of evolutionary format suggested in some Marxist historical theories. According to Touraine, "society is a system capable of producing, of generating its own normative guidelines instead of having them passed down via an order or a movement that transcends society—no matter whether one call it God, Spirit or History."[30] Touraine's "actionalist" sociology seems to free people not only from such "metasocial" controls,[31] but also from an oppressive false consciousness. While it is still a *class* that takes action in the new era of social movements, it is a class bearing "its own consciousness" free of central control by the "party" or by "revolutionary intellectuals."[32]

Pierre Bourdieu has also undertaken to rescue actors from what he calls the "mechanical determinations" specified by "social physics." Confronting the problem of unintended consequences of intentional human action, he refuses to accept an explanation that depends on "automatic behaviors" or simple reactions to objective conditions. Bourdieu is keenly aware, however, of the traps hidden in an empty doctrine of free will, and he cannot rely on anything like that to explain the reality of social outcomes of individual acts. Yet he will not abandon the individual to a status of automaton. He tries, then, to escape the "spurious alternatives of social physics and social phenomenology" through his conception of a *habitus*. He defines *habitus* as a system of dispositions that people shape in themselves, either individually or collectively, by an internalization of their experienced history. Sets of dispositions incline people to act in ways conducive to certain outcomes, but they do not rigorously dictate or produce a course of action, nor are they to be regarded as anything externally imposed on people. The dispositions, in this view, must be there and be effective, and yet acting subjects have had a part in shaping them. "The *habitus,*" Bourdieu says, "contains the solution to the paradoxes of objective meaning without subjective intention."[33]

All of this does much to reinstate human beings as effective social actors, and yet Touraine and Bourdieu leave an impression that their actors do not quite know what they are doing. When Touraine denies the sociological propriety of any opposition between objective determinants and subjective will or intention, and when Bourdieu refuses to choose between system attributes and human intentions for explanation of social facts, they leave a gap in our understanding of social causation that is not really bridged by somewhat obscure references to "relational analysis"[34] or "the principle of dialectical relationship."[35] Touraine evidently does not like to use the words "individual" or "person"; the actor in a social movement is always a "class actor" struggling against a "class adversary," and actions themselves are to be grasped only as a product of social relations in which actors "find themselves"—to their surprise, as it were. Sociology studies nothing but "systems of social relations," and "historicity" (the self-production of society) is a characteristic of a society, not the work of an actor. And although Touraine has endowed the class involved in social movements with consciousness, he reminds us that "every sociologist knows that the meaning of behavior cannot be conflated with the consciousness of actors" even though the actors themselves so account for their conduct. The implication here that actors do not really know what they are doing is made quite explicit by Touraine in another context: it is the sociologist, he notes, who arrives at "an understanding of social relations that cannot be grasped by the actors themselves but make it possible to explain and predict their conduct in defined conditions." And sociologists cannot, of course, rest with mere understanding; they must "intervene directly. It is only through them that actors can rise from one level of social reality to another and go from response and adaptation behavior to behavior of project elaboration and conflict. It is only if the researchers intervene actively and personally to draw actors towards the most basic relations in which they are engaged that the latter will be able to stop defining themselves only by responding to the established order."[36]

This disquieting relegation of human actors to a status of at least relative ignorance and the drawing of a line between sociologist-humans and nonsociologist-humans are also parts of Bourdieu's estimate of the human condition. "It is because," he says, "agents never know completely what they are doing that what they do has more sense than they know." The *habitus* as a set of dispositions to act in certain ways is, in his judgment, something much different from accumulated knowledge or wisdom derived from experience and consciously used by persons for guidance in their conduct. It is "embodied history, internalized as *a second nature* and so forgotten as history." When people pursue certain marriage or fertility or educational policies, then, they are neither making rational calculations nor simply yielding to some economic determinism. They are manifesting "dispositions inculcated by conditions of existence, *a kind of socially constituted instinct* which causes objectively calculable demands of a particular form of economy to be experienced as an *unavoidable call of duty or an irresistible impulse of feeling.*"[37] Bourdieu's language here suggests that he is using *habitus* as a near equivalent of natural propensities, such as are used to account for patterned behavior in animals or humans. In seeking to escape the subjective-objective opposition, he appears to leave little of the subject to figure in social action.

Bringing people back in to an analysis of social action must involve more than simply placing them on the scene to go through motions. They must be given something to do, deliberately, consciously, and on their own, not just as puppets moved by strings of instinct and impulse or, worse, by academic experts claiming a monopoly of knowledge. To bring people on the scene and have them strive intentionally for goals never realized and accomplish only unanticipated results is a depressing affront to human worth.[38] It would seem better, indeed, to attribute inadvertence to structures, or to impersonal historical forces, or to the providence that has served to comfort people in the grip of mysterious happenings. People should be brought back in not just to produce social action, but also to understand and to mean what they are doing. To suggest that people can make their own history, but cannot know what they are doing—

cannot decide what kind of history to make, and then make it—is to see human activity as a poor and pointless thing. John Calvin at least allowed people the power and the freedom to decide to do evil and then to do it.

The point is made by Anthony Giddens when he calls for recognition of the causal significance of human intentions, reasons, and motives in any explanation of social activity. The existence of knowledge about social life is not, in itself, any guarantee of human freedom; there must, Giddens reminds us, be purposeful application of such knowledge in a context of rational reflection by all human actors about their conduct. Nor is it enough, he argues against the "normative functionalism" of Durkheim and Parsons, to represent social interaction as guided mechanically by motives or "internalized" values. This denies the "negotiated and contingent" character of human action and ignores its subjectivity: "the reflexive monitoring of conduct that distinguishes specifically human behaviour from that of the animals."[39]

When Giddens turns, then, to acknowledge and deal with the fact of society as collectivity, it is with due caution to avoid losing sight of "the necessary centrality of the active subject." Structure exists, and institutional analysis has a part in analysis of human social conduct, but we should, he argues, be careful of a point of view that displays structure as a constraint on action. Giddens seeks, rather, to activate structure itself, to view it as a process of "structuration" in which primacy is reserved for acting persons.[40] How successful this effort to reconcile human freedom and the aims of sociological analysis might be will depend on different readings, but Giddens has surely proceeded with unusual sensitivity about the predicament in which social science has placed humankind.

Other sociologists share his concern. Jack Gibbs has recently chided sociologists for their "indifference to the purposive quality of human behavior." Their preoccupation with latent functions and unintended consequences, he observes, reflects their uneasiness about dealing with the "internal behavior" (such as purpose) associated with manifest functions. Their basic fear, as George Homans suggested earlier, is reductionism.[41] James Coleman has voiced similar concerns about a sociology that takes the human being simply as "a socialized element of a social system," thus eliminating questions about strains between humans and society or the freedom of people to act as they will. Coleman proposes to construct a theory of "purposive action" as opposed to theories that seek the causes of action not in the intentions of persons but in forces external to them or in their unconscious. While his brand of "methodological individualism" does not at all abandon the notions of a social system or of emergent phenomena resulting from interaction among individuals, Coleman nonetheless professes (somewhat self-consciously perhaps) to take "a humanistically congenial image of man" as opposed to "a fatalistic view of the future, in which humans are the pawns of natural forces."[42]

Favorable pictures of human beings such as these emphasize that people are capable of effective, conscious action in their social life and cultural work. They show people as able to construct reasons for doing things and then to act on those reasons with power to shape their lives accordingly. These are indeed liberating visions. But there is in other sectors of modern social theory an extension of this image along lines we have seen suggested in Renaissance and Enlightenment beliefs. This is the idea that humans are not just *capable* of shaping themselves as social and cultural beings, but that they *must* do so. They cannot live as other than social and cultural beings, and there is no source of society or culture outside themselves.

An example of this kind of thinking is found in Herbert Blumer's symbolic interactionism. In developing George Herbert Mead's idea of the "self," Blumer undertook at the outset to counter social scientific notions of a social structure or system in which people only react or adapt to features of their physical and social environment. There is, of course, a structure to human society. This is especially clear in what Blumer called "settled" societies, where joint action is repetitive and stable, resulting in what we call social order and culture: so we find rules, norms, values, roles, status positions, rank orders, institutions, and institutional relations. But these structures do not determine action; on the contrary they are products of actions that are constructed by humans. Nor does action issue from inherent, ineluctable psychic forces. Action, whether it be self-interaction or interaction with others, involves persons in constant appraisals or interpretations of their own and others' feelings, of expectations and goals, of objects and situations that they confront in daily living. In the complex social psychology of Mead, the fact that humans are objects to themselves makes them special kinds of actors in the world. In Blumer's words "the process of self-interaction puts the human being over against his world instead of merely in it, requires him to meet and handle his world through a defining process instead of merely responding to it, and forces him to construct his action instead of merely releasing it."[43]

This is what the animals on Circe's island knew so well, and this is why they were not inclined to leave a kind of life in which no such demands were made on them. And it is because humans are in this situation that Pico della Mirandola knew they could not be expected to act like angels and might, in fact, act like beasts. As Blumer put it: "The fact that the human act is directed or built up means in no sense that the actor necessarily exercises excellence in its construction. Indeed, he may do a very poor job in constructing his act. . . . He may do a miserable job in constructing his action, but he has to construct it."[44]

The significant feature of these ideas for an image of human nature is that they give humans something to do—something very important they are *required* to do—in the daily course of their lives. Here is a myth, if you will, that activates people and makes them, as selves, responsible for their conduct.[45]

Jurgen Habermas has taken this Meadian description of the acting individual as a key concept in his elaborate attempt to escape the stultifying effects of systems theories and the depressing outlook of some recent variations on Marxist thinking. He confronts directly the theoretical problem that arose from the eighteenth-century conception of two worlds of human social life: one in which things were comprehended and controlled rationally and consciously by people, and another in which results were produced (by the "market," for example) without the intentions of human actors.[46] For methodological purposes Habermas designates these aspects of society as a "lifeworld" and a "system." For the "system" Habermas makes the usual specifications of unintended consequences and latent functions that can be comprehended "from the standpoint of an observer who objectivates the lifeworld," but not "from the perspective of participants."[47] When society is conceived as a lifeworld, however, Habermas accepts what he calls the "fiction" that people are autonomous and capable of responsible participation in adjusting their actions to those of others by free and rational communication about "criticizable validity claims." Although he is quick to add in this context that people "never have their action situations totally under control," Habermas has here presented a myth that humans "acting autonomously" can participate in a social life that "takes place with the will and consciousness of adult members."[48]

Given his careful consideration of the necessary conditions for effective social communication, Habermas obviously is very far from saying that systematic imperatives render people's control of their social life impractical. Marx's degree of optimism about the role of human agency in transforming bourgeois society might be attenuated somewhat in Habermas's inability to discern clearly a group of people who will "activate" the "conflict zone" in today's society,[49] but his broad vision of actual human power is still strong and detailed.

The enabling of human beings by requiring them to act by virtue of their very humanity is an image that has thus survived in modern thought. This reassertion of human dignity in the study of social and cultural life can perhaps serve to rescue men and women from the helplessness to which a misguided social science has helped to condemn them.

CHAPTER SIX

For an Open Image of Humanity

THE RECORD of myth making about the nature of humans shows that this can be a dangerous affair. Some conceptions of human nature have blocked inquiry into the actual causes of social and cultural phenomena, have denied people the power of self-direction, and have been used to justify the authority of those who would control the lives of men and women thus deprived of freedom. Experience should make us wary of any attempt to spell out what is natural for humans.

And yet our lives are poor and meaningless if we do not conduct ourselves with some vision of what we can do. We have to ask, therefore, what an appropriate image of humanity might be.

[1]

There is a sense in which we can speak legitimately of a human nature. Humans, like other animals, have characteristic biological features. Differences among creatures in these respects result from an evolutionary process of descent with modification, and taxonomists identify configurations of traits that characterize distinct kinds of organisms. Any given configuration or structure is referred to by that vague, omnibus term "nature."[1] Thus a hermit crab, a civet cat, a wildebeest, and a human each is said to have a nature that biologists describe, although the descriptions are by no means engraved on stone and the lines between kinds are often redrawn. One can, however, pick up a manual such as François Bourlière's *Natural History of Mammals* and find a list of kinds with descriptions of what constitutes them as kinds.

All of this is straightforward enough. There is no special difficulty in regarding one animal as having a civet nature and another a human nature; there is a civet kind and a human kind. As long as we are talking about objective organic products of evolutionary change that serve as taxonomic criteria there is no problem. Some theologians do not like to hear civets and humans mentioned in the same breath, and some biologists are not convinced that people are quite ready to see themselves as animals, but these are not serious matters.

Difficult questions do arise, however, when the human species is observed to display a wide range of quite different social and cultural features alongside the uniform organic characters that identify it as one. It is this situation that led Ortega y Gasset to say that humans have no nature, but only history.[2] He was not denying, of course, that humans possess the specific organic qualities described by biologists, but he was noting the impossibility of explaining different human histories in terms of those common biological features. He was denying, that is, that humans have a "natural history" as far as their social and cultural life is concerned.

The fundamental limitation of any concept of human nature, in the sense the term is used by most biologists, is that it fails to capture the very characteristic of humans that, from a broader perspective, distinguishes them from other species: the human capacity for devising and acting out, from time to time and place to place, radically different modes of life. It is not "in human nature" for people to make and live by certain social arrangements or to shape and use certain cultural items. The biological concept of human nature therefore catches practically no part of what is most distinctive and important about human beings. When the zoologist Marston Bates asked "what is natural to man?" he could only answer, in all candor, "very little, as far as I can see."[3]

Might it be proper, then, to say it is human nature to be opportune in inventing new ways of life, to possess an open agenda for action, to make different histories? That is a plausible description, but we should avoid an implication that this human display of versatility is a constant expression of an organic or genetic constitution instead of the occasional and historically conditioned activity that it is. It would be better to reserve the term human nature to mean those biological features that are taken by taxonomists to distinguish Homo sapiens from other species. And to bear in mind how very little, indeed, that says about humankind.

It has been urged that besides the obvious need and use for a biological concept of human nature we require some practical determination of human traits before we can go about our daily interaction with each other and before we can engage in the conduct of social and political life in general. If we are to interpret what others say, read their gestures, put ourselves in their place in order to understand their doings, anticipate how they will react to our acts, or know what people are likely to do in given situations, then do we not need to know something about human nature? Do we not expect different things from humans than we expect from other animals—our dogs and cats, for instance—and is this not because humans are naturally different from dogs and cats? Should we not know something about the fallibility of human reason, the reality of selfishness, the strong urges to which people are subject, and their weakness of will before we embark on programs of social reform or political control? Is it not a mark of effective social leaders and successful politicians that they know what can and cannot be expected of human nature, just as it is the naiveté of bunglers in this regard that involves them in futile quests of utopia?

There is substance in these observations, no doubt, and they make sense so long as they do not lead to that common hypostatization of people's habits that takes us beyond a commonsense, practical level into heights of so-called theory about the binding force of inherent and ineluctable human traits. Maslow, for example, seems to have gone beyond the point he meant to make when he said, "even the year-old child, has a conception of human nature, for it is impossible to live without a theory of how people will behave."[4] Granted that Mary and Johnny soon learn what to expect of Mama, and how that differs from what can be counted on from Grandpa or Auntie. But to speak of a child, or anybody else, having a conception or theory of human nature conveys an impression of an abstract humanity with behavior potentials that can be known by people for the purpose of guiding action in general. What we know about people in our daily lives is always knowledge about particular persons. Similarly, the leader who seems to have a feel for gauging the public is actually making judgments informed by his knowledge of how certain people have responded to certain situations on specific occasions under given conditions. That kind of information can be extensive, based upon a wide experience and careful consideration of cases, but nothing is added to it by calling it a knowledge of human nature.

When we move from the area of private and public conduct to the professional study of human activity a need for human nature theory can again be claimed. Sociologists often make the general point that they must proceed with some kind of at least implicit assumptions about what people are like, and this is usually the case. In a search for or a weighing of evidence that might explain a given human act one proceeds with clues provided at least by introspection, probably by some order of information gathered from similar contexts, and possibly by systematic comparisons of typical acts in typical situations. Whatever the level of sophistication or methodical rigor, the fact that the investigator is a human seeking understanding of other humans introduces a condition of inquiry different from investigation of nonhuman phenomena—a condition of some familiarity with what is to be expected of human beings. This was a premise that underlay Vico's argument for the possibility of a science of human affairs: humans can understand what other humans have done because they can put themselves in the place of other acting men and women in a way they can never put themselves in the place of gravitation or friction or any other natural force. The same proposition was a basis for Max Weber's *verstehende* sociology: we can understand human actions by entering empathetically into the situation of other humans and coming to see what their intentions might have been in so acting. In some instances this can be achieved rationally, while in other action situations an appreciation of emotional context can be achieved only by "sympathetic participation" or identification with actors.

Now it might seem to be an inescapable implication of both Vico's and Weber's method that we can understand other people because we are *like* them, and when we press the question of what the likeness *is* we appear to be close to what is involved in traditional depictions of human nature. But clear differences should be noted.

First, neither Vico nor Weber undertook anything like a formal specification of traits, drives, forces, or dispositions that were supposed to produce or account for a corresponding set of actions. It was precisely in opposition to such an eighteenth-century physical science approach that Vico advanced his case for a "new" science, and Weber followed in Vico's footsteps here as elsewhere.

Second, and more important, Vico and Weber, and those who have worked in their tradition of comparative history, speak of human beings only in a context of actual situations and conditions. Abstract human nature always gives way to concrete human actions, reactions, and reflections in richly detailed historical settings. Vico's insistence on getting inside a historical scene and viewing it from the perspective of the participants, and Weber's requirement of dealing with historical "individuals" rule out grand deductions from principles of human nature. Generalization is not at all precluded, but so far as what can be said generally about why people acted as they did, only quite guarded empirical statements about types of acts in types of situations are in order.

But what most distinguishes the Vichian and Weberian kind of outlook from that of traditional human nature theorists is that the former does not involve the mistake of reifying or hypostatizing ways of human acting and then using them as explanatory devices to account for historical actions. Weber was aware that human beings had commonly reacted to anxiety-producing situations with frantic activities apparently unrelated to the specific situations themselves, but he did not fall into the error of saying that capitalism had been caused by a human anxiety complex or by any other postulated psychic force.

John Dewey pointed out the danger involved in letting descriptive classifications become causative things in themselves: "The tendency to forget the office of distinctions and classifications and to take them as marking things in themselves, is the current fallacy of scientific specialism. It is one of the conspicuous traits of highbrowism, the essence of false abstractionism. This attitude which once flourished in physical science now governs thinking about human nature."[5] The absurdity of saying, for example, that people do evil things because they are by nature evildoers, is apparent if we would stop to think how little sense it would make for a biologist to say that skunks discharge fetid secretions because they are by nature fetid-secretion-dischargers. Yet this is a common feature of human nature mythologies, and it arises, as we have seen, from the circumstance that we have been unable to discern and identify a force in human nature apart from the exertion of the force. The conceivable range of qualities that can be put into human nature is limited, therefore, only by interpretations of the entire scope of human experiences, and there are no reliable criteria for distinguishing nature and historical experience. As Dewey went on to remark in this connection, we have reason to respect Thomas Hobbes's judgment that people in seventeenth-century England had good grounds for being fearful, but Hobbes gave us no evidence that fearfulness is an identifying feature of human nature.

While students of human social life must, then, work with knowledge of how people have come to act as they have acted in particular situations, the rich complexity of the situations must be respected as well as the fact that human action is more than a manifestation of inward forces or a simple reaction to circumstances. Reflection on the situation and, of course, reflection on past actions in past situations, can, from time to time, make for quite different human reactions to similar conditions.

Human nature theory has also been defended on the ground that it is actually no more than recognition of the reality of selfhood, of human authenticity, of human integrity—a specification of what it means to be a human being, and so a set of indications of how people should be regarded and treated by each other. To proceed either in social action or social inquiry without some picture of human nature, it is argued, amounts to leaving people as such out of consideration and thus disregarding a necessary basis of moral judgment. If men and women are no more than a reflection of their circumstances—nothing in themselves—then they can be helpless products of circumstances created or controlled by persons whose objectives have nothing to do with the needs or wishes of those they dominate. The ability of authoritarian political regimes in the post–World War I era to manipulate the beliefs and actions of people in incredibly revolting ways has led some thinkers to question the desirability of unbounded human malleability and to seek an affirmation of strong and intractable qualities in human nature that can be relied on to limit what people can be made to do.[6] Confronted with the awful fact that people were actually induced to cooperate with their tormentors in Nazi concentration camps, Barrington Moore felt it necessary to postulate a powerful sense of injustice in human nature, for only this seemed to promise escape from the inevitability of the depths to which people could be led by mere conditioning.[7] A similar attempt to escape, via human nature arguments, from the moral relativism implicit in social determinism is evident in the arguments of psychoanalytic scholars who see culture's formative effects resisted by stubbornly unyielding natural propensities or needs in people.[8]

Such arguments, though reasonable and moderate, eventually must face troublesome questions of just how essential traits of human nature are to be ascertained and, if they are not, what purpose is served by an appeal to human nature. As Salkever put it, the recalcitrant human needs that are assumed to exist "can be seen only indirectly"—that is, can be confirmed only by observation of efforts to achieve something—and therefore cannot be known precisely. Moore clearly searched for evidence of a sense of injustice only in empirical-historical data on what people have avoided or sought. The futility of moving from such observations of human acts to conclusions about human needs and then to causal attribution of the acts to the needs is bothersome enough without the difficulties of inference from acts to needs. A generalization about an observed course of human activity is neither confirmed nor enhanced by a statement that it is human nature to act that way.

If it be said that the reference to human nature in these instances is no more than a manner of speaking about what we have learned concerning widespread kinds of human social and cultural doings, then we should be reminded how easily this manner of speaking has been accompanied by an assumption that what is widespread or common or universal is natural—is, in this case, "in human nature," and therefore necessary. And in the instances considered here the soft denial of reductionism or of any intention to postulate peremptory instincts in the human make-up only presses the question of why, then, the concept of a human nature is broached at all. To say that it is human nature to act in such and such a way, and then to say that people are not obliged to act in that way, is really to abandon any claim to natural law status for the generalization. There is a good deal of eating your cake and having it too in this practice of explanation by appeal to a human nature that can break its own rules.

It appears, then, that social scientists can depend on no conception of human nature other than that supplied by traditional biologists. That is not very helpful, and it is understandable that more would be hoped for from such fields as sociobiology and psychobiology. Meanwhile, students of human social and cultural life must work with more or less systematized information about what people's actions and reactions have been in typical situations, just as anyone in the course of daily life must act on the same sort of intelligence. To proceed as if the situation were otherwise would be epistemologically unsound and morally reckless. Human activity cannot be realistically regarded as a product of natural forces.

We do need, nevertheless, something more than this practical knowledge of what people generally do and do not do. We need ideas about what people can do, an enabling and liberating and compelling vision of human capacity and responsibility. In the light of Western experience in self-reflection, what might be an appropriate myth about ourselves?

[2]

A basic element in an open image of humanity is the belief that people can make their social and cultural life by their deliberate activity—by their conscious and intentional action. When we produce historical consequences in a state of absentmindedness we are engaged in meaningless action. We have to believe ourselves able to act meaningfully if we are to act at all. Deliberation requires a creation and use of symbols as part of the planning of actions for achievement of ends. This distinguishes deliberate work from the behavior of other animals, whose work is often skilled and intricate and even social in the sense of being objectively coordinated.

By recognizing, cultivating, and facilitating this ability to shape our social lives and perform our cultural work, we express ourselves in art, language, science, politics, religion, economics—all the forms of historical doing. Humans are unique in this basic fact of their *activity*. And it is not that they are just relatively more active than other animals. Other animals are not active at all in the sense that humans can conceive, initiate, and carry out basic changes in the pattern of what they do, how they live from time to time and place to place.

As Cassirer warned us, we can forget this distinctive feature of Homo sapiens because modern thinking about humanity is unfortunately skewed by a prevalent acceptance of the notion of continuity in nature.[9] When Thomas Huxley, in 1863, undertook to determine "man's place in nature," he was sure that an enlightened view depended on realizing that men and women are animals—fantastically intelligent animals, granted, but still animals by virtue of their place in an evolutionary process by which all organisms had come to be, a process that required an absolute qualitative continuity in its products.[10] Darwin took pains to show, in his *Descent of Man*, how the human being is connected by a finely graded series of variations to all other members of the organic world. From amoeba to human there could be no gap in the spatial series of organic differences just as there had been no gap in the temporal series of changes that had brought about the different array of organisms. People, Darwin granted, are superior to animals in many ways, but the difference is always a matter of degree; incipient forms of any human quality can be found in other animals. Humans are to be understood, then, in terms of their origin in a universal evolutionary process, and it would be the height of folly and vanity, in this Darwinian view, to claim for them any distinct or separate place. As Montaigne had put it earlier, all nature is one, and "Man must be forced and lined up within the barriers of this organization."[11]

Although Darwin believed that he must resist any wedge of creationism or supernatural intervention in natural processes, the theoretical necessity for absolute continuity in evolution was never clear. The notion antedated Darwin considerably, and it is apparently not required in some modern versions of the theory of evolution. But it is a mainstay (although not always made explicit) of a human nature myth that submits people to bonds of instinct and genetic disposition.

Comparison of humans and other animals has long been a popular pastime and a fetching literary device for satire and moral discourse. Recent refinements in ethological technique have greatly extended what we know about animal behavior, and this new knowledge has been put to service in the game of discovering similarities between humans and animals and in the more serious endeavor to depict all nature as one. In some cases people are presented as inferior to animals in many respects and are reduced to nonentities who can appropriately be submitted to control by the few who have managed to escape biological degradation.[12]

The moral implications of asserting the essential similarity of people and other animals should make us wary, but the myth should also be recognized as a plain misapprehension of the human condition. Likening men and women to apes or geese is really an absurd way to seek knowledge about people, for it obscures rather than reveals what is distinctive and important about humans— their activity. Quite apart from the moral messages of competing myths, then, there are good reasons for accepting the argument that humans as symbol makers and users act intentionally to build cultural lives in a way that is radically different from other animal behavior.

But while we bear in mind the distinguishing role of symbols and intentions in the doings of people, we might better grasp the full significance of human action by recognizing that this activity is its own source, its own constructor. Specific human ways of life are *consequences* of specific human activity. This is the solemn meaning of the proposition that people make their own histories—and must make their own histories for better or worse. What we *do* results in the *way* we produce our food and shelter. Our acts, physical and mental, have outcomes in how we produce a next generation of persons, what kind of god or set of principles we construct for our guidance, how we get knowledge about doing any of these things, and how we express artistically our thoughts and feelings about our experience of life. Other animals, of course, follow patterns of doing things, but their doing them has little or no effect on how they do them— the behavior does not change by doing. It does not change from one historical time to another. It does not have consequences for future behavior. Other animal behavior patterns come to be by the evolutionary process of natural selection of controls, not by historical processes.

Human societies differ from so-called animal societies in that the former have "conscious" histories. Learning is passed on in various ways, but acquisition of a consciousness of the past is something distinct. Awareness of the past in a historical sense affects human conduct in ways quite unknown among other animals. Some human behaviors are evolutionary products, but the great variety of kinds of activity in Homo sapiens, which we observe in different historical times and different geographical places, is evidently a result of human activity itself, not of different or changing genetic dispositions, not of different human natures.

We need think only of the contrast between human and other animal innovation to realize the significance of human consequential activity. Intriguing accounts of chickadees learning to pry caps off milk bottles or of a macaque genius who discovered she could wash sand off food with sea water can be seized to establish our kinship with other creatures only by ignoring the fantastic range and richness of human culture histories. It was acting people who devised the machinery, rationalized the manufacturing process, mobilized a captive work force in cities, and took all the other measures necessary for an industrial revolution that has fundamentally transformed human existence. Inquiring scholars learned languages, studied texts, discovered intellectual traditions other than their own, and so created an Italian Renaissance. Individual people undertook to harness a new source of energy, encapsulate it in a bomb, and drop it on Hiroshima and Nagasaki, thus ushering in a nuclear age the full consequences of which are still unknown. Human beings decided to enslave other humans and in one case transported them to a land dedicated to freedom, thus creating a dilemma yet to be solved by human action. People, by their planning and thinking and tinkering devised an astonishingly fast and extensive means of calculating, storing, and transmitting information and so inaugurated an era of computers in which the lives of men and women—and children—are different from anything hitherto known. Thus humans shape their ways of life by their own activity.

The observation that such profound consequences of human acts have often been a surprise to actors who had no intention of producing them cannot in itself alter the fact that human action did produce the consequences. Belief in the operation of other agencies—an invisible hand or providence or their surrogates—is not sustained by rational inquiry and should not be resorted to for evading responsibility or for concealing covert action. The fact that we often do not achieve what we deliberately set out to accomplish, or even that we create what we seek to avoid, is commonly taken to imply that we have little power to control our lives. But what must be remembered is that nothing else is going to control our lives for us. There is no escape from the fact that our situation at any time is a set of consequences of our acts. So if, as often happens, those consequences are not the ones we want, our only recourse is to purposefully recast our acts, not to pretend that some alien force produced the consequences, and not to hope, or pray, that it might do better for us in the future. A decision that people can act *intelligently* to achieve results must be an integral part of the myth that the conditions of human life are the consequences of human action.

[3]

But if people, by their deliberate activity, can and do create their social and cultural lives, a question remains as to the extent of their freedom to do so and the possible limits within which they must work. Are there constraints in the conditions of action, and are there limits imposed by humanity itself?

Karl Marx said that people do make their own history but they do not make it under conditions of their own choosing. Serious obstacles arising from past human activity appeared to him to limit what can be accomplished at any given moment. While Marx refused, then, to recognize impediments to action in History or other such fictions, he could still see people caught in circumstances that could render some of their strivings futile.

It is easy to elevate this prudent respect for circumstances into a debilitating conviction that we are pawns caught in a game where the moves are controlled by impersonal forces—structures, institutions, system requirements, and the like. It seems unlikely that Marx the revolutionary could let himself get caught in that trap. For while it is important to recognize that human action always is taken in a context of conditions, some of human origin and some of physical setting, dealing with conditions must be accepted as part of any course of action. If people who have gone before you acted in ways that created difficulties for the achievement of your goals, that is just one of the conditions of your action. Part of the problem of effective activity in pursuit of chosen ends is, of course, to proceed with an awareness of circumstances and a strategy for dealing with them. To give conditions of action a conceptual status of determinants is misleading, however, for that can encourage the familiar retreat into pretending that objective situations rather than people make decisions and dictate lines of conduct. That is part of a philosophy of history that relegates human beings to roles of uncomprehending spectators, much less effective actors. Practical recognition of conditions that are judged to make one course of action more likely than another to yield a wanted outcome is just a requisite of rational conduct. An open image of human beings must, then, picture them as more than reflections of the conditions of action.

It must also present them as free from those internal constraints and compulsions that Western tradition has put into their "nature." We have come to view ourselves as weak and as driven by destructive forces. We have denied ourselves the dignity of being able to lead lives we choose. We have tended to confuse humility with passivity and loss of nerve. We have on the one hand disclaimed responsibility for our shortcomings by attributing them to forces beyond our control, while on the other we have told ourselves that anything like virtuous action must depend on special dispensation. We have thus represented human moral action, the doing of both evil and good, as somehow detached from our conscious being, as if our acts were not really our own. We have, in sum, become alienated from ourselves.

The point is not to replace this negative and derogatory characterization of humanity with a set of positive and noble qualities, for that would be only to carry on in the habit of regarding people as natural objects moved by inherent forces to behave in prescribed ways. There is little point in trying to say what people are in essence. Men and women are, above all else, what they do, and their doing is not a function of their constitution, not a result of qualities in their make-up. Colin Turnbull puts it well: "What is special about humanity is not what man *is,* but what he *can* be; humanity is a whole range of potential granted us by our enormous adaptability and our intellect. Our nature is determined by what we do with that potential, not the other way around. And, wherever there is choice, man ultimately is what he wants to be."[13]

Humans, as Pico della Mirandola told us, should regard themselves as capable of anything. We should take that as a moral premise; we should decide that we are like that. The Socratic belief in human dignity is a confidence in the ability of people to use their reason to reveal the way to a life of virtue. Jurgen Habermas's hope for the fruit of reasoned communication in a free society is a similar vision. How the Socratics and Habermas came to hold that conception of humanity is a legitimate question, but it was not, in any event, a discovery of the nature of humans. It was rather a decision, a working assumption for the moral conduct of life.

The belief that people can form myriad ways of life, free from impediments or requirements in human nature, is supported in fact by the record. The range of different cultures and social arrangements that have been devised by people defies attempts to specify boundaries to human activity. Notions about genes or instincts or commands from dark recesses of the soul setting limits to forms of cultural expression and social interaction run up against this panorama of differences. When attempts are made to capture the diversity in encompassing concepts of universal requisites the necessarily vague generality of such formulas makes them almost meaningless. The differences are real and rich and cannot be reduced to mere variations on recipes engraved in human nature. If there be such a thing as human nature, then as C. Wright Mills remarked, its limits are "frighteningly broad."[14]

* * *

Mill's reference to a frightening human potential should remind us that a belief in human dignity—a belief that we can control our lives—is a challenging rather than a comforting proposition. When we speak of human versatility and power we must recognize that people can use, and have used, this capacity to serve both rational and nonrational ends, to produce and to destroy, to do both good and evil things. The idea of human dignity is commonly dismissed by sophisticates as starry-eyed optimism or naiveté or a refusal to acknowledge the reality of the human tragedy. But a myth that gives power to humans, far from painting a rosy picture of their situation, demands that they act without reliance on sources outside themselves, with full responsibility for their action, and with no assurance of salvation or damnation mediated by powers beyond their own. The question is not whether such a view flatters humankind, but whether it can help people to leave the false comfort of a belief that places their fate in the operation of incomprehensible alien forces and to move out on their own.

The choice to stay in or move out of a lifetime of natural shelter is the one presented so vividly to the humans-turned-animals on Circe's island. Leading a human life is a difficult matter. We lack the set of internal directions that other animals can rely upon. Even in small matters of daily conduct we can be so puzzled and embarrassed about what we should do that we see the point of Samuel Butler's quip about life being "like playing a violin solo in public and learning the instrument as one goes on." In the larger arenas of public life, difficulties must be faced with nothing like social and cultural "faculties" to help us. Unlike ants, we must fashion our social life and do our cultural work from scratch. And the difficulty is compounded by the fact that we must not only make our lives and thus our selves whatever they are to be, but we have to decide as well what we want to be. In this way the human being is, indeed, *causa sui* to the second power." [15]

Leaving Circe's island involves facing life without reliance on either natural or supernatural guidance, but it also means abandoning illusions about "history" accomplishing anything on its own. A myth that presents people as able to make their history must also present them as obliged to do so, obliged in the sense that there is nothing else to do the job. There is no escape from either the consequences of action or the necessity for action.

We can be sustained in this trying situation only by a conviction, a buoyant myth if you will, that we are capable of making our histories despite all difficulties. An essential part of an appropriate image of humanity denies any alienating doctrine that deprives humans of worth, dignity, and power and gives over history making to any other agency.

This picture of what people are like cannot properly be regarded as a boastful myth derived from human vanity or marred by dangerous hubris. There is nothing here of Nietzschean bombast about superman. A claim that men and women can by their effort of will and reason shape their lives and do their work seems as modest as it is necessary when we bear in mind the greatness of their task. Awareness of the difficulty of life and of the need for care is fitting, but humility at the cost of confidence and courage is grievous surrender to the challenges of a human existence of activity.

Notes

INTRODUCTION: The Human Nature Question

1. President Ronald Reagan's addresses to the International Association of Chiefs of Police in New Orleans, excerpted in the *New York Times,* 29 September 1981, and to the National Association of Evangelicals in Orlando, Florida, 8 March 1983, excerpted in the *New York Times,* 9 March 1983.

2. Georg Hegel, *The Logic of Hegel,* trans. from the *Encyclopaedia of the Philosophical Sciences* by William Wallace (Oxford: Clarendon Press, 1874), 213.

3. The point was made nicely by Leon Eisenberg in "The *Human* Nature of Human Nature," *Science* 176 (14 Apr. 1972): 123–28.

4. Among serious endeavors: E. O. Wilson, *Sociobiology: The New Synthesis* (Cambridge: Belknap Press of Harvard University Press, 1975); *On Human Nature* (Cambridge: Harvard University Press, 1978); Richard D. Alexander, *The Biology of Moral Systems* (Hawthorne, N.Y.: A. de Gruyter, 1987).

CHAPTER 1: Images of Adam's Offspring

1. I depend here chiefly on the detailed and broadly informed scholarship of Elaine Pagels, especially in her *Adam, Eve, and the Serpent* (New York: Random House, 1988).

2. Quoted by Pagels, *Adam, Eve, and the Serpent,* 168 n. 19.

3. In addition to Pagels, see for a thorough exposition of Saint Augustine's depiction of human nature, Jimmy Joseph Christiana, *Human Nature Theory and the Natural Law Tradition* (Ph.D. diss., University of California, Berkeley, 1985), 146–209.

4. W. E. H. Lecky, *History of the Rise and Influence of the Spirit of Rationalism in Europe,* 2 vols., rev. ed. (New York: D. Appleton, 1900), 1:360–63.

5. Stephan Chorover, *From Genesis to Genocide: The Meaning of Human Nature and the Power of Behavior Control* (Cambridge: MIT Press, 1979).

6. A serious Jesuit priest once told me (as if it were an accepted fact) that Augustine's attack on Pelagius involved nothing more than putting an upstart British monk in his place when he challenged a Roman position.

7. Pagels, *Adam, Eve, and the Serpent,* 117–50.

8. Herschel Baker, *The Image of Man: A Study of the Idea of Human Dignity in Classical Antiquity, the Middle Ages, and the Renaissance* (New York: Harper, 1961 [originally published as *The Dignity of Man* by Harvard University Press, 1947]), 200. There are astonishing differences of interpretation among experts in recounting this whole story. Compare, for example, Charles Trinkaus, *In Our Image and Likeness,* 2 vols. (Chicago: University of Chicago Press, 1970). Baker and Trinkaus seem to be talking about quite different people when they discuss Augustine. There was, of course, an "early" and "late" Augustine and an Augustine who spoke of Adam before and of Adam after the Fall.

9. Patristic, as well as ancient and medieval, sources of Renaissance humanism have been pointed out by Paul Oskar Kristeller, *Eight Philosophers of the Italian Renaissance* (Stanford: Stanford University Press, 1964); *Renaissance Concepts of Man, and Other Essays* (New York: Harper & Row, 1972). Kristeller makes the important point that we tend to forget the breadth and richness of our humanistic heritage, leaving ourselves with "nothing but the bleak alternative between science and religion" (*Eight Philosophers,* 141). Major writings of Renaissance humanists are available in *The Renaissance Philosophy of Man,* ed. Ernst Cassirer, Paul Oskar Kristeller, and John Herman Randall, Jr. (Chicago: University of Chicago Press, 1948).

10. For a detailed and appreciative analysis of Ficino, see Paul Oskar Kristeller, *The Philosophy of Marsilio Ficino,* trans. Virginia Conant (New York: Columbia University Press, 1943).

11. The version quoted here is from Pico della Mirandola, *On the Dignity of Man,* trans. Charles Glenn Wallis (Indianapolis: Bobbs-Merrill, 1965), 3–17. Pico's *On Being and the One,* trans. Paul J. W. Miller, and *Heptaplus,* trans. Douglas Carmichael are also published in this volume. For an analysis and appreciation of Pico, see Ernst Cassirer, "Giovanni Pico della Mirandola: A Study in the History of Renaissance Ideas," parts 1 and 2, *Journal of the History of Ideas* 3 (Apr.–June 1942): 123–44, 319–46.

12. Pico della Mirandola, *Heptaplus,* 123–26.

13. For Pico della Mirandola's antecedents and many-sidedness, see Trinkaus, *In Our Image and Likeness,* chap. 10. Augustine's account of pre-Fall Adam yields a very favorable view of man, of course, but that all but disappears in the anti-Pelagian writings. Scholarly dispute over the novelty of Renaissance humanist ideas need not detain us here. Pico's *Oration* can be regarded simply as one given myth of human nature.

14. The translation used here: *The Circe of Signior Giovanni Gelli of the Academy of Florence, consisting of ten dialogues between Ulysses and several men transformed into*

beasts, satirically representing the various passions of mankind and the many infelicities of human life, trans. Thomas Brown, corrected and retranslated in part by Robert Adams (Ithaca: Cornell University Press, 1963). Gelli lived from 1498 to 1563; the *Circe* was written in 1548.

15. Ibid., 174.

16. Ibid., 172. Only one former woman appears (as a doe) among the animals in the dialogues. Her reasons for declining to return to human form rest on the unjust treatment of women by men; she feels better off among male deer.

17. Many Renaissance thinkers were involved in a similar contradiction when they accepted an astrology that depicted astral influences on human activity. Pico della Mirandola, significantly, saw the difficulty and urged his fellow humanists to forego both astrology and the pagan conception of Fortune or Fate (Kristeller, *Eight Philosophers,* 68). For a general discussion of the problem, see Hélène Vedrine, *La Conception de la Nature chez Giordano Bruno* (Paris: Libraire Philosophique J. Vrin, 1967), chap. 2; Dorothea Waley Singer, *Giordano Bruno: His Life and Thought,* with annotated translation of his work, *On the Infinite Universe and Worlds* (New York: Henry Schuman, 1950), 74–79, 263–64, 269.

18. Theodore Spencer, *Shakespeare and the Nature of Man,* 2d ed. (New York: Macmillan, 1961). A similar theme was developed earlier by E. M. W. Tillyard, *The Elizabethan World Picture* (London: Chatto & Windus, 1958 [1943]).

19. John Herman Randall, Jr., *The Making of the Modern Mind,* rev. ed. (Boston: Houghton Mifflin, 1940), 226. Randall went on to remark, "the absolute insignificance of man before the mighty and relentless will of Calvin's stern deity seems pomp and glory compared with the place to which he has been relegated by modern astronomy."

20. The general reaction against Renaissance humanism is described by Hiram Hayden, *The Counter-Renaissance* (Gloucester, Mass.: Peter Smith, 1966 [1950]).

21. William J. Bouwsma, *John Calvin: A Sixteenth-Century Portrait* (New York: Oxford University Press, 1988).

22. Martin Luther, *On the Bondage of the Will,* in *Luther and Erasmus: Free Will and Salvation,* ed. and trans. E. Gordon Rupp et al. (Philadelphia: Westminster Press, 1969), 328–29.

23. In John Calvin, *Institutes of the Christian Religion.* The edition cited here is the two volumes edited by John T. McNeill and translated by Ford Lewis Battles (Philadelphia: Westminster Press, 1960). The *Institutes* first appeared in 1535; there were several revisions and enlargements.

24. Calvin, *Institutes* I:xv.8; II:i.7,8.

25. Ibid. II:i.8; ii.22; iii.5.

26. Ibid. II:iii.5; I:xvi.5; II.i.8; III:xiv.5.

27. Ibid. II:v.19. Specific consideration of natural and supernatural human endowments remaining after the Fall is given in II:ii. Bouwsma notes that

Calvin was equivocal about the post-Fall human condition and warns against being misled by Calvin's harsh rhetoric, which might have been in large part an expression of his deep concern about the reality of sin generally and especially in his own time (Bouwsma, *John Calvin*, 116, 141–45). This leaves the question of how Calvin accounted for the reality of sin.

28. Calvin, *Institutes* II:ii.21; v.19; ii:24; III:ii.10. Calvin's argument that altruistic behavior cloaks selfish motives and that the motives are often or usually unconscious is strikingly repeated in current sociobiological discourse. See, for example, Richard Dawkins, *The Selfish Gene* (New York: Oxford University Press, 1976); Richard D. Alexander, *Darwinism and Human Affairs* (Seattle: University of Washington Press, 1979), 275–76; Edward O. Wilson, *On Human Nature* (Cambridge: Harvard University Press, 1978), chap. 7. Protestant theology and science are reconciled.

29. *Institutes* II:ii.19.

30. Ibid. I:xvi.1–3, 5.

31. Ibid. xvi.6,8; xvii.1.

32. Ibid. II:iv.8.

33. Ibid. III:xxiii.7. Calvin's careful demolition of the case for free will is in II:v.

34. Ibid. II:ii.7.

35. Ibid. III:xx.6–7.

36. Ibid. II:iii.7, 10; II:v.1; III:xxiii.2; II:iii.11. Calvin deals with predestination in III:xxi–xxiv.

37. Ibid. I:xvii.3–11.

38. Need for the church is, of course, implied by what has been said regarding humans. Because of our "ignorance and sloth" God has provided the church, with its pastors and teachers, to show us the way to God (ibid. IV.i.1).

39. Baker, *The Image of Man*, 320, and references cited there.

40. Montaigne, *Apology for Raimond Sebond*, in *The Essays of Montaigne*, ed. and trans. E. J. Trechman (New York: Modern Library, 1946 [1580]), 374, 378, 525.

41. Robert Burton, *The Anatomy of Melancholy*, ed. Paul Jordan-Smith and Floyd Dell (New York: Tudor, 1958), 146, 617, 624, 638, 658 et passim.

42. François de La Rochefoucauld, *The Maximes of the Duc de La Rochefoucauld*, trans. Constantine Fitzgibbon (London: Allan Wingate, 1957 [various editions from 1665 to 1678]).

Fitzgibbon reflects the "realism" of our own time when he says, "From the viewpoint of the mid-twentieth century [the Maximes] must seem very mild and moderate, as well as extremely sensible" (ibid., 20).

43. Jean de La Bruyère, *Characters*, trans. Henri van Laun (London: Oxford University Press, 1963 [1688]), 174.

CHAPTER 2: Shaftesbury and Mandeville

1. See Samuel I. Mintz, *The Hunting of Leviathan* (Cambridge: Cambridge University Press, 1962), esp. chap. 5.

2. *The Cambridge Platonists*, ed. Gerald R. Cragg (New York: Oxford University Press, 1968), 63, 64, 66, 411.

3. Ibid., 245, 297, 306

4. Ibid., 422. On this point see James Deotis Roberts, Sr., *From Puritanism to Platonism in Seventeenth-Century England* (The Hague: Martinus Nijhoff, 1968), 123–32.

5. See John K. Sheriff, *The Good-Natured Man: The Evolution of a Moral Ideal, 1660–1800* (University: University of Alabama Press, 1982).

6. Shaftesbury, *Characteristics of Men, Manners, Opinions, Times*, ed. John M. Robertson (Indianapolis: Bobbs Merrill, 1964 [1711]), 1:73

7. Ibid. 1:77–81.

8. Ibid. 1:64.

9. Ernest Tuveson, "The Importance of Shaftesbury," *English Literary History* 20 (1953): 267–99.

10. Shaftesbury, *Characteristics* 2:68–69.

11. Ibid. 1:237–338, "An Inquiry Concerning Virtue or Merit." See esp. 255, 336–38.

12. Ibid. 1:74–75. Here Shaftesbury anticipates James Madison's argument, in *The Federalist*, no. 10, that an encompassing union of people can be jeopardized by their very tendency to combine in smaller groups—a tendency that Shaftesbury regarded as an "abuse or irregularity" of the natural social impulse.

13. It is difficult to know when to take Mandeville seriously; it is possible that he did not know when he was serious. He probably came to overstate his case as he became embroiled in controversy. He was plainly having fun in some of his writing and had a good idea of what would attract attention and would sell. It is not necessary here to pursue these questions because Mandeville obviously has been taken seriously by others; his influence is clear.

14. Bernard Mandeville, *The Fable of the Bees*, part 2 (London: J. Roberts, 1729), 133. The principal themes of the *Fable* were first published in verse form, *The Grumbling Hive: Or, Knaves Turn'd Honest* (London: Ballard, 1705). This was followed in 1714 by a prose exposition; the edition cited here is *The Fable of the Bees: Or, Private Vices, Publick Benefits, with an Essay on Charity Schools, and a Search Into the Nature of Society*, 3d ed. (London: J. Tonson, 1724). This is often referred to as vol. 1 and the part 2 cited above as vol. 2.

15. *Fable* 1:37, 10–11, 105–6, 255 et passim.

16. Ibid. "The Preface."

17. Ibid. part 2:18, 156.

18. F. B. Kaye, "Introduction," to *Mandeville's Fable of the Bees* (Oxford: Claren-

don Press, 1924), I:xcviii-ciii, cxxix, cxl; F. A. Hayek, "Dr. Bernard Mandeville," *Proceedings of the British Academy* 52 (1966): 125, 141; Thomas A. Horne,
The Social Thought of Bernard Mandeville (New York: Columbia University Press,
1978), chap. 4.

19. Mandeville, *A Modest Defense of Publick Stews: Or, An Essay upon Whoring,
as it is now Practis'd in these Kingdoms,* Written by a Layman (London: A. Moore,
1724).

20. *Fable* 1:411, 253.

21. Ibid. 1:86–91.

22. Ibid. 1:82.

23. Ibid. 1:95.

24. Ibid. 1:89.

25. Mandeville notes in this connection that what is most odious to people is
a clue to what is most common—a good Freudian observation.

26. Discussion of pride runs through the whole of Mandeville's work; it is
specifically the focus of Remark M in *Fable* 1:125–39.

27. Mandeville's evolutionism appears especially in *Fable* 2:141–56. This feature of his work has been noted with approval by Louis Schneider, *Paradox
and Society: The Work of Bernard Mandeville* (New Brunswick, N.J.: Transaction
Books, 1987), and by M. M. Goldsmith, *Private Vices, Public Benefits: Bernard
Mandeville's Social and Political Thought* (Cambridge: Cambridge University Press,
1985). Goldsmith provides an excellent bibliography of Mandeville studies.
This and other features of Mandeville's relationship to modern social theory
are discussed in Hector Monro, *The Ambivalence of Bernard Mandeville* (Oxford:
Clarendon Press, 1975); Irwin Primer, ed., *Mandeville Studies: New Explora-
tions in the Art and Thought of Dr. Bernard Mandeville (1670–1733)* (The Hague:
Martinus Nijhoff, 1975); and Richard I. Cook, *Bernard Mandeville* (New York:
Twayne, 1974).

28. See "An Enquiry into the Origin of Moral Virtue," in *Fable* 1:27–44, 428.

29. This problem in *Fable* is examined by Goldsmith, *Private Vices, Public Benefits,* 61–64. Goldsmith sees the clever politician as only a rhetorical device in
Mandeville.

CHAPTER 3: A Secular Idea of Providence

1. Shaftesbury, *Characteristics of Men, Manners, Opinions, Times,* ed. John M.
Robertson (Indianapolis: Bobbs-Merrill, 1964 [1711]), 1:78.

2. Bernard Mandeville, *A Letter to Dion,* ed. Bonamy Dorbree (Liverpool:
University Press of Liverpool, 1954 [1732]), 32–33, 36–37. This was rationalized by the familiar device of saying that providence uses "Engines" to perform
its work, "visible" means for accomplishing its ends. Mandeville's use of provi-

dence is discussed and put in context by J. A. W. Gunn, "Mandeville and Wither: Individualism and the Workings of Providence," in *Mandeville Studies: New Explorations in the Art and Thought of Dr. Bernard Mandeville (1670–1733)*, ed. Irwin Primer (The Hague: Martinus Nijhoff, 1975), 98–118. Gunn offers detailed evidence that Mandeville freely used the "language of divine providence" to "detail the spontaneous operation of unintended consequences."

3. For some of Vico's references to providence, see *The New Science of Giambattista Vico*, revised translation of the 3d ed. (1744 [1st ed. 1725]), ed. and trans. Thomas Goddard Bergin and Max Harold Fisch (Ithaca: Cornell University Press, 1968), 3–4, 24, 62, 70, 92, 100–103, 121, 425; see also Fisch's "Introduction," xxxii–xxxiii, xliv–xlv. The relation of human and providential factors in history has received wide attention in Vichian scholarship. See, for example, Leon Pompa, *Vico: A Study of the New Science* (New York: Cambridge University Press, 1975), chap. 5; Maeve Edith Albano, *Vico and Providence* (New York: Peter Lang, 1986); Isaiah Berlin, *Vico and Herder* (New York: Vintage Books, 1977), 37, 52, 80–82, 113–14; James C. Morrison, "How to Interpret the Idea of Divine Providence in Vico's New Science," *Philosophy and Rhetoric* 12 (Fall 1979): 256–61; A. Robert Caponigri, *Time and Idea: The Theory of History in Giambattista Vico* (Chicago: Regnery, 1953).

4. Turgot's influential contributions on the subject were contained in two essays he wrote as a young man, "Tableau Philosophique des Progrès Successifs de l'Esprit Humain" (1750), and "Plan de deux Discours sur l'Histoire Universelle" (1751), in *Oeuvres de Turgot*, ed, Gustave Schelle (Paris: Librairie Felix Alcan, 1913), 1:214–35, 275–323.

5. Condorcet, *Esquisse d'un Tableau Historique des Progrès de l'Esprit Humain*, in his *Oeuvres Complète* (Paris: Henrichs, 1804), 8:15–16, 39–40 et passim.

6. Quoted by Helmut A. Pappe, "Enlightenment," in *Dictionary of the History of Ideas* (New York: Charles Scribner's Sons, 1973), 2:92–93.

7. Auguste Comte, "Plan of the Operations Necessary for Reorganizing Society," in *System of Positive Polity* (London: Longmans, Green, 1877 [1854]), 4:555–56.

8. Immanuel Kant, "Idea for a Universal History with Cosmopolitan Intent" (1784), in *The Philosophy of Kant*, ed. Carl Friedrich (New York: Modern Library, 1949), 116–31. This essay must be read, of course, with an understanding that Kant did not intend here to depict any actual history but rather to find a standpoint from which to launch humanity on a quest for moral autonomy. Endowing humans with Shaftesbury's qualities of sociability was not enough for that purpose. Cassirer finds some eighteenth-century elements in Kant's essay along with a portent of the nineteenth-century quest for a radical human freedom. Ernst Cassirer, *Kant's Life and Thought*, trans. James Haden (New Haven: Yale University Press, 1981), 223–26.

9. David Hume, "Of the Dignity and Meanness of Human Nature," in *Essays*

Moral, Political, and Literary, ed. T. H. Green and T. H. Grosse, 2 vols. (New York: Longmans, Green, 1898), 1:155–56.

10. Hume, *A Treatise of Human Nature,* ed. L. A. Selby-Bigge, P. H. Nidditch, 2d ed. (Oxford: Clarendon Press, 1978), 415. And even reason "is nothing but a wonderful and unintelligible instinct in our souls," 179.

11. Alexander Pope, "An Essay on Man," in *Alexander Pope, Selected Poetry,* ed. Martin Price (New York: New American Library, 1970), Epistle 2, lines 107–8.

12. Ibid., lines 53–54.

13. Hume, *Treatise,* 528–29.

14. Hume, *Essays* 1:294–95.

15. Ibid. 1:117–22. On the method of counterpoise and a reminder of James Madison's use of the argument in *Federalist* no. 10, see Arthur O. Lovejoy, *Reflections on Human Nature* (Baltimore: Johns Hopkins, 1961), 38–53. The practicality of Hume's interest in unintended consequences is evidenced by his concern in this instance with the counterpoise of power in the House of Commons by the Crown's control of appointments to important offices. Thus, what at first glance might appear to be "corruption and dependence" actually works for the preservation of mixed government.

16. Hume, *Essays* 1:299–309, "Of Refinement in the Arts."

17. Adam Smith, *The Wealth of Nations* (1776), in *A Library of Universal Literature* (New York: P. F. Collier and Son, 1901), 16:56–57.

18. Ibid. 17:160–61. In his *Theory of Moral Sentiments* (London: Henry G. Bohn, 1853 [1759]), 264–65, Smith called on an invisible hand to make sense of benefits to the poor resulting from indulgence in luxury by the rich; in this context "providence" is also credited.

19. Smith, *Wealth of Nations* 18:23–24.

20. Louis Schneider has provided a most useful collection of excerpts from the works of the Scots on this and other topics: *The Scottish Moralists on Human Nature and Society* (Chicago: University of Chicago Press, 1967).

21. Thomas Reid, *The Works of Thomas Reid,* preface, notes and supplementary dissertations by William Hamilton, 2 vols. Vol. 1, 7th ed.; vol. 2, 6th ed. (Edinburgh: Maclachlan and Stewart, 1872, 1863), 1:545–60.

22. Adam Ferguson, *Principles of Moral and Political Science,* 2 vols. (Edinburgh: printed for A. Strahan and T. Cadell, London, and Creech, Edinburgh, 1792), 1:27–28.

23. Ibid. 1:43.

24. Ibid. 1:313–14.

25. Ibid. 1:258–65.

26. Adam Ferguson, *An Essay on the History of Civil Society,* 2 vols. (Edinburgh: Edinburgh University Press, 1966 [1767]), 7.

27. Ibid., 182, 122–24.

28. See Isaiah Berlin, "The Counter-Enlightenment," in *Dictionary of the History of Ideas* (New York: Charles Scribner's Sons, 1973), 2:100–112.

29. Lord Monboddo (James Burnet), *Of the Origin and Progress of Language*, vol. 1, 2d ed. (Edinburgh: 1774), 16, 24ff., 185, 209ff.; and *Antient Metaphysics*, 6 vols. (Edinburgh: 1779–99), 6:280.

30. Reid, *Works* 2:523, 622.

31. Ibid. 2:525, 543, 637. See chap. 7, "Of the Extent of Human Power," 2:527–30.

32. Ibid. 1:481–89.

33. Ferguson, *Principles* 1:179.

34. Ibid. 1:200–201. Ferguson had earlier, at the conclusion of his *Essay on the History of Civil Society*, 279–80, warned against pleading a "fatality in human affairs."

35. Ferguson, *Principles* 1:54, 225.

36. Ibid. 1:131, 71, 95.

37. Ibid. 1:151–53.

38. Ibid. 1:242–46; 2:424–25.

39. Ibid. 1:176–78, 180–81, 184. Ferguson's belief that people must be spurred to action by difficulties in their lives is similar to the view expressed by Kant in the Fourth Principle of his *Idea for a Universal History*, but with this important difference: where Kant found the difficulties in human nature itself, Ferguson located them in external circumstances and specifically excluded human nature. Part of the difficulty confronting people results, he noted, from an *absence* in human nature of attributes that help other animals survive.

CHAPTER 4: Freud's Scientific Mythology

1. For a disturbing consideration of such questions, see Philip Rieff, *Freud: The Mind of the Moralist*, 3d ed. (Chicago: University of Chicago Press, 1979), chap. 3, "The Hidden Self."

2. Ludwig Wittgenstein, *Wittgenstein: Lectures and Conversations*, ed. Cyril Barrett (Oxford: Blackwell, 1966), 51–52.

3. Albert Einstein and Sigmund Freud, *Why War?* (International Institute of Intellectual Cooperation, League of Nations, 1933), 47. And, a page later, "From our 'mythology' of the instincts we may easily deduce a formula for an indirect method of eliminating war."

4. Sigmund Freud, *Beyond the Pleasure Principle* (New York: W. W. Norton, 1989), 40.

5. Sigmund Freud, *New Introductory Lectures in Psychoanalysis* (New York: W. W. Norton, 1965), 84.

6. For the following discussion, see ibid., 91–95.

7. James Strachey said (ibid., 96 fn.) that what Freud wrote here "is almost wholly derived from *Beyond the Pleasure Principle*," but although Freud made his usual reference there to a "rich fund of analytic experience," the first twenty-

five pages of that work contain a quite limited amount of empirical data, and on page twenty-six he announced, "What follows is speculation, often far-fetched speculation," and later (71–72), "it is impossible to pursue an idea of this kind except by repeatedly combining factual material with what is purely speculative and thus diverging from empirical observation."

8. These were not offhand remarks by Freud that might be considered to have no relation to the practical matter of what he really thought of human beings. In a supposedly pragmatic discussion of the problem of human warfare, Freud said, "With the least of speculative efforts we are led to conclude that this [destructive] instinct functions in every living being, striving to work its ruin and reduce life to its primal state of inert matter" (*Why War?* 45).

9. See, for example, the remarks in Freud, *Group Psychology and the Analysis of Ego* (London: Hogarth Press, 1955), 122, 135.

10. Freud, *The Interpretation of Dreams*, 3d ed., trans. A. A. Brill (London: George Allen and Unwin, 1932), 254–55.

11. Rieff, *Freud*, 34.

12. Freud, *Moses and Monotheism*, trans. Kathleen Jones (New York: Vintage Books, n.d.), 127–28.

13. Examples: Freud, *Civilization and Its Discontents* (New York: W. W. Norton, 1962), 89–91; *Moses and Monotheism*, 68,71, 117; *Future of an Illusion* (New York: W. W. Norton, 1961), 17, 42–43; *Beyond the Pleasure Principle*, 44. "Freud never gave up his belief—I am tempted to say faith—that the parallel he drew between Fechner's ideas in physics and his own in human psychology was not really a parallel but an actual proof that his concept of the mental apparatus and its energy was actually the same as Helmholz' and Fechner's ideas about physical energy" (Gregory Zilboorg, "Introduction" to *Beyond the Pleasure Principle*, xxviii–xxix).

14. Adolf Grunbaum, *The Foundations of Psychoanalysis: A Philosophical Critique* (Berkeley: University of California Press, 1984) presents a carefully argued and painstakingly documented case against the acceptability of Freud's analytic data. Grunbaum's indictment of psychoanalytic methodology is specific and temperate almost to a fault, and he acknowledges that Freud was more aware than many of his disciples of the possible contamination of clinical data.

15. Freud, *Moses and Monotheism*, 7, 98, 120.

16. Freud, *Future of an Illusion*, 28, 36.

17. Arnold J. Toynbee, *Civilization on Trial* (New York: Oxford University Press, 1948), 11–12.

18. In *Wittgenstein*, ed. Barrett, 52.

19. Freud, *Civilization and Its Discontents*, 40.

20. Freud, *Future of an Illusion*, 7–8.

21. Freud, *Why War?* 49–50.

22. Freud, *Future of an Illusion*, 49.

23. Freud, *New Introductory Lectures*, 92; *Civilization and Its Discontents*, 56–57, 90.

24. Freud, *The Resistances to Psychoanalysis*, in *The Standard Edition of the Complete Psychological Works of Sigmund Freud*, ed. and trans. James Strachey (London: Hogarth Press, 1961), 19:217–18, 221.

25. Hilary Callan, *Ethology and Society: Towards an Anthropological View* (Oxford: Clarendon Press, 1970), 161.

26. See the remarks of Lawrence K. Frank in "Man's Changing Image of Himself," *Zygon* 1 (June 1966): 162.

27. John Calvin, *Institutes of the Christian Religion*, ed. John T. McNeill, trans. Ford Lewis Battles (Philadelphia: Westminster Press, 1960), 3:2.10.

28. See, for example, Reinhold Niebuhr, *The Nature and Destiny of Man* (New York: Charles Scribner's Sons, 1964), 1:252; Paul Ricouer, "'Original Sin': A Study in Meaning," trans. Peter McCormick, in *The Conflict of Interpretations: Essays in Hermeneutics*, ed. Don Ihde (Evanston: Northwestern University Press, 1974), 269–86.

29. Freud lapsed into religious symbols on occasion—for example, "The manifestations of a compulsion to repeat . . . exhibit to a high degree an instinctual character and, when they act in opposition to the pleasure principle, give the appearance of some 'daemonic' force at work" (*Beyond the Pleasure Principle*, 41).

30. Sharon MacIsaac, in *Freud and Original Sin* (New York: Paulist Press, 1974), 1. 3, concludes from a comprehensive reading of Freud that he helps to explicate and fill out the doctrine of original sin, which revealed "the human condition as diseased by a cumulative, pre-deliberate perversity." MacIsaac is grateful to Freud for having provided the theology of sinfulness with a needed "empirical verification."

31. Niebuhr, *Nature and Destiny of Man* 1:255.

32. The mythical foundation for this fundamental contradiction is supplied by Freud largely in *Totem and Taboo*.

33. Freud, *New Introductory Lectures*, 86; *Instincts and their Vicissitudes*, in *Standard Edition* 14:122, 126; *On Narcissism*, ibid. 94–95. A comprehensive discussion of the possibilities of sublimation is not evident in Freud's work.

34. There is, Freud thought, "an active instinct for hatred and destruction," a "will to kill," a "lust for aggression" that might be diverted from expressing itself in war but cannot be suppressed entirely. *Why War?* 27, 40, 43, 47, 48.

35. The similarity between Freud and Calvin is here again impressive. Calvin also placed individuals beyond the reach of self-help and, so far as salvation is concerned, beyond the reach of anything but grace.

36. Nancy Chodorow, *The Reproduction of Mothering: Psychoanalysis and the Sociology of Gender* (Berkeley: University of California Press, 1978).

37. Rieff, *Freud*, 33–34, 56–64 et passim.

38. Freud, *The Ego and the Id* (New York: W. W. Norton, 1962), 46; *New Introductory Lectures*, 71: "Where id was, there ego shall be."

39. Freud, *Future of an Illusion*, 7.

40. Ibid., 55.

41. Ibid., 53–54.

42. Freud, *An Autobiographical Study*, in *Standard Edition* 20:72.

43. Freud, *Future of an Illusion*, 48–49. Emphasis added; he might have been wishing before, but now returns to the world of reality.

44. Ibid., 7.

45. Freud, *Civilization and Its Discontents*, 69; *Why War?* 47, 51–52.

46. Freud, *Future of an Illusion*, 5, 8–9.

47. Ibid., 79.

48. Ibid., 6–8, 64.

49. Frank J. Sulloway, in his *Freud, Biologist of the Mind: Beyond the Psychoanalytic Legend* (New York: Basic Books, 1979), traced in detail the contributions of Darwinian evolutionary biology to psychoanalytic theory (see esp. chaps. 7 and 10), but he did not deal with Freud's debt to nineteenth-century *cultural* evolutionism, a different intellectual tradition. Lamarckism, incidentally, was an integral part of cultural evolutionary thought; on this point see George W. Stocking, Jr., *Race, Culture, and Evolution* (New York: Free Press, 1968), chap. 10.

50. In addition to Frazer, Freud depended heavily on John Lubbock, Herbert Spencer, Andrew Lang, Edward Burnett Tylor, R. R. Marett, Wilhelm Wundt, Edward Westermarck, W. H. R. Rivers, Lewis Henry Morgan, J. J. Bachofen, and J. F. McLennan. See the "List of Works Referred To" in *Totem and Taboo* (New York: W. W. Norton, 1950), 162–67. Freud did not appear to be concerned about the method and assumptions of cultural evolutionism and showed little of the caution with which many of the evolutionist scholars presented their conclusions.

51. Freud, *Civilization and Its Discontents*, 92. For other hints about organic changes (organic repression) behind the alteration of cultural life, see ibid., 46–47 n. 1; 52–54 n. 3; *New Introductory Lectures*, 157–58.

52. Recognizing that people are "divided into leaders and led" by virtue of their "inborn and irremediable inequality," Freud pointed out that the vast majority "need a high command," "a superior class of independent thinkers . . . whose function it will be to guide the masses dependent on their lead." He saw little chance of success, however, for this indirect method of preventing war (*Why War?* 49–51).

53. Ibid., 53–54.

54. Freud's failure to explain the evolutionary process that produced an elite leaves it unaccounted for in much the same way that Calvin's chosen group could be viewed only as a product of God's inscrutable will.

55. Freud, *Civilization and Its Discontents*, 44.

56. Freud, *Why War?* 53.

57. Calvin quoted by William J. Bouwsma, *John Calvin: A Sixteenth-Century Portrait* (New York: Oxford University Press, 1988), 172; Montaigne, *Apology for Raimond Sebond*, in *The Essays of Montaigne*, trans. E. J. Trechman (New York: Modern Library, 1946), 388; E. O. Wilson, *On Human Nature* (Cambridge: Harvard University Press, 1978), 167.

CHAPTER 5: Social Science and Human Agency

1. For a rich and penetrating account of the movement in Western thought from the Reformation's theological determinism to the scientific revolution's mechanical determinism, see Herschel Baker, *The Image of Man* (New York: Harper, 1961 [1947]), and *The Wars of Truth* (Gloucester, Mass.: Peter Smith, 1969 [1952]).

2. The classic account of utilitarian positivism and the problems it bequeathed to nineteenth- and twentieth-century social thinkers is Elie Halévy's *The Growth of Philosophic Radicalism*, trans. Mary Morris (London: Faber & Faber, 1934).

3. For a summary exposition of these aspects of Comte's and Spencer's scientific program, see Kenneth Bock, *The Acceptance of Histories* (Berkeley: University of California Press, 1956), 5–13.

4. Although the general model of natural science was consciously aspired to in the study of social and cultural evolution, the specific Darwinian theory of organic evolution was not followed. Much of the work antedated Darwin; the basic ideas were already there in seventeenth- and eighteenth-century notions of progress; and social evolutionists spoke of a process quite different from Darwin's descent with modification. Darwin's language was later cited for support, but this was largely window dressing.

5. Talcott Parsons, *The Structure of Social Action: A Study in Social Theory with Special Reference to a Group of Recent European Writers* (Glencoe, Ill.: Free Press, 1949 [1937]), 396, 440, 467, 719 et passim. An analysis of this work as an effort to deal with the metaphysical problem of free will was made by Barclay DeLay Johnson in *Some Philosophical Problems in Parson's Early Thought* (Ph.D. diss., University of California, Berkeley, 1975).

6. George C. Homans, "Bringing Men Back In," *American Sociological Review* 20 (Dec. 1964): 809–18. Homans accused sociologists of actually having recourse to psychology when it comes down to saying why people really act the way they do, but "they keep psychological explanations under the table and bring them out furtively like a bottle of whiskey." For a more wide-ranging critique of structural-functional neglect of the human factor in history see Nancy DiTomaso, "'Sociological Reductionism' from Parsons to Althusser: Linking

Action and Structure in Social Theory," *American Sociological Review* 47 (Feb. 1982): 14–28.

7. The human brought back in by Homans was hardly the liberated person one might have expected, but one conditioned to behave pretty much as a Skinnerian creature.

8. Ralf Dahrendorf, "Homo Sociologicus," and "Sociology and Human Nature," in his *Essays in the Theory of Society* (Stanford: Stanford University Press, 1968), 19–106.

9. Marx and Freud are examples of the "behind-peoples'-backs" theme. Erich Fromm exploited it effectively in his *Beyond the Chains of Illusion: My Encounter with Marx and Freud* (New York: Simon and Schuster, 1962), chaps. 2 and 3.

10. Dennis Wrong, "The Oversocialized Conception of Man in Modern Sociology," *American Sociological Review* 26 (Apr. 1961): 183–93. Like the man brought "back in" by Homans, the person Wrong rescues from oversocialization is by no means free from other controls. "Powerful impulses," "strong instinctual motives," "material interests, sexual drives, and the quest for power" all appear still to move the individual who must live with "despair and darkness in his heart." Wrong believes, however, that the psychoanalytic view is less deterministic than the sociological.

11. Harold Garfinkel, *Studies in Ethnomethodology* (Englewood Cliffs, N.J.: Prentice-Hall, 1967), 67–71.

12. Norman P. Barry, *The Invisible Hand in Economics and Politics* (London: Institute of Economic Affairs, 1988), 27–28.

13. Frank H. Knight, *Risk, Uncertainty, and Profit* (New York: Augustus M. Kelley, 1964 [1921]), xlix, lx.

14. F. A. Hayek, *The Counter-Revolution of Science: Studies in the Abuse of Reason* (Glencoe, Ill.: Free Press, 1952), 80 et passim. It is ironic that Hayek sought, in good faith, to make this point in a context of defending human freedom. Analysis of unintended consequences of human action can, of course, be carried out without ideological baggage. A good example is Thomas C, Schelling, *Micromotives and Macrobehavior* (New York: W. W. Norton, 1978).

15. Robert E. Merton, "The Unanticipated Consequences of Purposive Social Action," *American Sociological Review* 1 (1936): 894–904; "Manifest and Latent Functions," in *Social Theory and Social Structure,* rev. and enlarged ed. (New York: Free Press, 1957), 19–84. Merton's choice of this Freudian terminology suggests, of course, a parallel between the ideas of an invisible hand and an unconscious that directs the conduct of humans to ends of which they are unaware.

16. Louis Schneider, *Paradox and Society: The Work of Bernard Mandeville* (New Brunswick, N.J.: Transaction Books, 1987); *The Scottish Moralists on Human Nature and Society* (Chicago: University of Chicago Press, 1967), xxxii–xxxiii.

17. Piotr Sztompka, *System and Function: Toward a Theory of Society* (New York: Academic Press, 1974), 120.

18. Neil Smelser and R. Stephen Warner, *Sociological Theory: Historical and Formal* (Morristown, N.J.: General Learning Press, 1976), 14–15.

19. Charles Taylor, *Hegel* (Cambridge: Cambridge University Press, 1975), 392–93, 419–20. The similarity of such a notion to the traditional idea of providence is noted by Taylor: "God's providence is the absolute cunning because he lets men follow their own passions and interests, but what happens is nevertheless the fulfilment of *his* intentions."

20. Merton, "Unanticipated Consequences," 898.

21. Colin Campbell, "A Dubious Distinction? An Inquiry into the Value and Use of Merton's Concepts of Manifest and Latent Functions," *American Sociological Review* 47 (Feb. 1982): 29–44.

22. Karl Popper, "Reason or Revolution?" *European Journal of Sociology* 11 (1970): 252–62; *The Open Society and Its Enemies* 4th ed., rev. (London: Routledge and Kegan Paul, 1962), 2:93–94, 323–24; "The Poverty of Historicism II," *Economica*, n.s., 11 (Aug. 1944): 122.

23. Karl Marx and Frederick Engels, *The Holy Family* (Moscow: Progress Publishers, 1975 [1845]), 110.

24. Karl Marx, *The Eighteenth Brumaire of Louis Bonaparte* [1852], in Robert C. Tucker, *The Marx-Engels Reader*, 2d ed. (New York: W. W. Norton, 1978), 595.

25. Karl Marx, *Capital: A Critique of Political Economy*, vol. 1 (Chicago: Charles H. Kerr, 1906), 13–14.

26. Karl Marx, *A Contribution to the Critique of Political Economy* (Chicago: Charles H. Kerr, 1904), 11.

27. Louis Althusser, *For Marx* (London: Allen Lane, 1969); Althusser, with Etienne Balibar, *Reading Capital* (London: New Left Books, 1970); Georg Lukács, *History and Class Consciousness: Studies in Marxist Dialectics*, trans. Rodney Livingstone (Cambridge: MIT Press, 1985); Antonio Gramsci, *Selections from the Prison Notebooks*, ed. and trans. Quinton Hoare and Geoffrey Norwell Smith (New York: International Publishers, 1971).

28. The question of whether Marx had a theory of human nature has been debated at length. See Vernon Venable, *Human Nature: The Marxian View* (New York: A. A. Knopf, 1945); Kate Soper, *On Human Needs: Open and Closed Theories in a Marxist Perspective* (Atlantis Highlands, N.J.: Humanities Press, 1981); Norman Geras, *Marx and Human Nature: Refutation of a Legend* (London: Verso Editions, 1983); W. Peter Archibald, *Marx and the Missing Link: "Human Nature"* (Houndmills: Macmillan, 1989).

29. Alain Touraine, *Return of the Actor*, trans. Myrna Godzich (Minneapolis: University of Minnesota Press, 1988). See also his earlier *The May Movement*, trans. F. X. Mayhew (New York: Random House, 1971), and *Sociologie de l'Action* (Paris: Editions de Seuile, 1965).

30. Touraine, *The Voice and the Eye: An Analysis of Social Movements*, trans. Alan Duff (Cambridge: Cambridge University Press, 1981), 2–7, 10, 14.

31. Touraine, *The Self-Production of Society*, trans. Derek Coltman (Chicago: University of Chicago Press, 1977), 48–49.

32. Touraine, *The Voice and the Eye*, 68–69.

33. Pierre Bourdieu, *The Logic of Practice*, trans. Richard Nice (Stanford: Stanford University Press, 1990 [1980]), 62. For a general discussion of the *habitus* concept, see part 1, chap. 3.

34. Touraine, *Return of the Actor*, 47.

35. Bourdieu, *Logic of Practice*, 140.

36. Touraine, *The Voice and the Eye*, 77; *Return of the Actor*, 49–51, 93; *Self-Production of Society*, 28, 64. Touraine is aware that his intervening sociologist might be regarded as another bearer of bureaucratic power, but he rejects such fears as groundless because sociologists have only ideas, which yield no power until embodied in a control apparatus (*The Voice and the Eye*, 219–20).

37. Bourdieu, *Logic of Practice*, 69, 56, 161 (emphasis added).

38. Raymond Boudon, for example, argues that social structures cannot explain unintended consequences, and he seeks to restore the free individual as an agent. But the "freedom" here appears to be a freedom to act perversely in ways comprehensible only by sociologists, not freedom to avoid undesired results or freedom from bondage to a social life where you do not know what is going to happen when you act in such and such a way. Raymond Boudon, *The Unintended Consequences of Social Action* (New York: St. Martin's Press, 1982).

39. Anthony Giddens, *Studies in Social and Political Theory* (London: Hutchinson, 1977), 107, 125, 129.

40. Ibid., 117–18, 125–30.

41. Jack P. Gibbs, *Control: Sociology's Central Notion* (Urbana: University of Illinois Press, 1989), 192–93.

42. James S. Coleman, *Foundations of Social Theory* (Cambridge: Belknap Press of Harvard University Press, 1990), 2, 5, 17–18, 31. It is not surprising that these views elicited reservations from his colleagues. His "individualistic" orientation seemed to one to put in question the possibility of a generalizing social science; and doubts were expressed about the place he gave to reason in human action at the expense of affect, feeling, and emotion (review by Neil Smelser in *Contemporary Sociology* 19 [Nov. 1990]: 778–83). Harrison C. White noted that Coleman seemed to shrug off "the awful grip of chance and the arbitrary on human affairs" (ibid., 783–88).

43. Herbert Blumer, *Symbolic Interactionism: Perspective and Method* (Englewood Cliffs, N.J.: Prentice Hall, 1969), 63–64.

44. Ibid., 64, 15.

45. Ann Swidler activates people in their dependence on culture by representing the cultural milieu as only a repertoire or "tool kit" from which indi-

viduals must choose items they judge suitable for use on specific occasions; thus the image of the cultural "dope" is avoided ("Culture in Action: Symbols and Strategies," *American Sociological Review* 57 [Apr. 1986]: 273–86).

46. Jurgen Habermas, *The Theory of Communicative Action*, vol. 2: *Lifeworld and System*, trans. Thomas McCarthy (Boston: Beacon Press, 1987), 202.

47. Ibid., 232–33.

48. Ibid., 149.

49. Jurgen Habermas, *Toward a Rational Society*, trans. Jeremy J. Shapiro (Boston: Beacon Press, 1971), 120. Thomas McCarthy has commented on this problem in his *Critical Theory of Jurgen Habermas* (Cambridge: MIT Press, 1978), 385–86.

CHAPTER 6: For an Open Image of Humanity

1. Sixty-six different usages of the word "nature" have been identified by A. O. Lovejoy and George Boas, *Primitivism and Related Ideas in Antiquity* (New York: Octagon Books, 1980), 447–56.

2. José Ortega y Gasset, *History as a System, and Other Essays towards a Philosophy of History* (New York: Norton, 1961), 217.

3. Marston Bates, *Gluttons and Libertines: Human Problems of Being Natural* (New York: Random House, 1967), 226. Some biologists have argued that humans do indeed have a nature that shapes their social and cultural life—that there is a natural human social history. This argument runs into the facts of social and cultural diversity, which are met with (1) a judgment that the diversity is unimportant, or, (2) a suggestion that there are different natural kinds of people. The second point revives the old case for a racial explanation of social and cultural differences. E. O. Wilson tried to deal with this "delicate question" in a letter to the *New York Times Magazine* (30 Nov. 1975): 86; in his *Sociobiology: The New Synthesis* (Cambridge: Belknap Press of Harvard University Press, 1975), 550; and *On Human Nature* (Cambridge: Harvard University Press), 42–43, 46, 48, 50. Another approach to a biological explanation of sociocultural life is to look for "culture" among nonhuman animals, apparently on the premise that this would make a biological account of culture among humans more plausible. See, for example, W. H. Thorpe, *Animal Nature and Human Nature* (Garden City, N.Y.: Anchor, 1974), 244–45; John Tylor Bonner, *The Evolution of Culture in Animals* (Princeton: Princeton University Press, 1980), 171–85.

4. Abraham Maslow, "The Need for a Mature Science of Human Nature," in *Human Nature: Theories, Conjectures, and Descriptions*, ed. John J. Mitchell (Metuchen, N.J.: Scarecrow Press, 1972), 6.

5. John Dewey, *Human Nature and Conduct* (New York: Henry Holt, 1922), 131–32.

6. See, for example, Maurice Mandelbaum, *History, Man, and Reason* (Baltimore: Johns Hopkins University Press, 1971), 161–62, 370–71.

7. Barrington Moore, Jr., *Injustice: The Social Bases of Obedience and Revolt* (White Plains, N.Y.: M. E. Sharpe, 1978).

8. A temperate example of the argument is Donald L. Carveth, "The Disembodied Dialectic: A Psychoanalytic Critique of Sociological Relativism," *Theory and Society* 4 (Spring 1977): 73–102. Others include, Stephen G. Salkever, "Beyond Interpretation: Human Agency and Slovenly Wilderness," in *Social Science as Moral Inquiry*, ed. Norma Haan et al (New York: Columbia University Press, 1983), 195–217; Anthony Leeds, "Sociobiology, Anti-Sociobiology, Epistemology, and Human Nature," in *Methodology, Metaphysics, and the History of Science*, ed. Robert S. Cohen and Marx W. Wartofsky (Dordrecht, Holland: D. Reidel, 1984), 215–34; Kate Soper, *On Human Needs: Open and Closed Theories in a Marxist Perspective* (New York: Humanities Press, 1981); Adam Scheff, *Alienation as a Social Phenomenon* (Oxford: Pergamon Press, 1980). I am indebted to Alessandro Ferrara and Randy Baker for illuminating conversations on the relevance of human nature theory to avoidance of moral relativism.

9. Ernst Cassirer, *An Essay on Man: An Introduction to a Philosophy of Human Culture* (Garden City, N.Y.: Doubleday, 1954), see esp. 279–81. My general debt to Cassirer is evident in much of what follows.

10. Thomas Huxley, *Man's Place in Nature, and Other Anthropological Essays* (New York: D. Appleton, 1896).

11. Montaigne, *Apology for Raimond Sebond*, in *The Essays of Montaigne*, trans. E. J. Trechman (New York: Modern Library, 1946), 388.

12. For a striking indictment of Konrad Lorenz in this matter, see the late Bruce Chatwin's review of *The Year of the Greylag Goose*, in *New York Review of Books* 26 (6 Dec. 1979): 8–9. For a broader treatment of monism see the excellent work cited by Chatwin: Daniel Gasman, *The Scientific Origin of National Socialism: Social Darwinism in Ernst Haeckel and the German Monist League* (London: MacDonald, 1971).

13. Colin Turnbull, "Human Nature and Primal Man," *Social Research* 40 (1973): 530.

14. C. Wright Mills, *The Sociological Imagination* (London: Oxford University Press, 1967), 6.

15. Ortega y Gasset, *History as a System*, 202.

Index

KENNETH BOCK is a professor emeritus of sociology at the University of California, Berkeley. He is the author of *The Acceptance of Histories* (California, 1956) and *Human Nature and History* (Columbia, 1980).